D1097660

Geographical Location

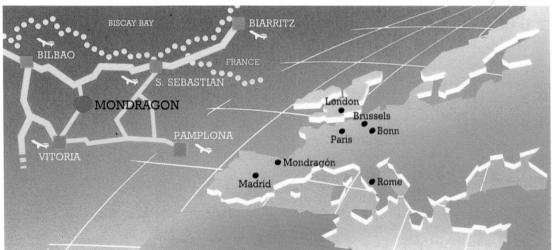

Located in the Basque Country, no more than 100 kms. from the French border, the Cooperatives of the MCC occupy a privileged position between the Iberian Peninsula and the rest of Europe.

This positive geographical situation is complemented by a good motorway network, three airports, with Biarritz airport in France close by, and two high capacity commercial sea ports: Pasajes and Bilbao, the latter being the port with most goods traffic in Spain.

THE MONDRAGON COOPERATIVE EXPERIENCE

**MONDRAGON
CORPORACION
COOPERATIVA**

CONTENTS

Don José María Arizmendiarrieta

"*Hand in hand, of one mind, renewed, united in work, through work, in our small land we shall create a more human environment for everyone and we shall improve this land.*

We shall include villages and towns in our new equality; the people and everything else: "Ever forward".

Nobody shall be slave or master of anyone, everyone shall simply work for the benefit of everyone else, and we shall have to behave differently in the way we work. This shall be our human and progressive union - a union which can be created by the people".

Perhaps Don José María Arizmendiarrieta's last piece of writing a few days before his death

INTRODUCTION

TO THE READER

This book is an attempt to give an account of *the social and economic experience* applied to enterprises, which embodies the **Mondragón Cooperative Group**.

In view of this aim I have tried to avoid expressing excessively abstract ideas and doing exhaustive research work, tasks which should remain in the hands of specialists in the fields of sociology and enterprise management.

In trying to find a way to offer practical information what will surely happen is that many readers will feel that there is insufficient detail, because they are familiar with the Experience from within or they know, from having practised the cooperativism of Mondragón, that there were other important facts and influences, which are not highlighted.

Others, however, who, although forming part of the system, are unfamiliar with its long course of development, will discover that its beginnings were very simple and owed much to reasons now lost in the mists of time and the shifting nature of society.

Whilst working on the book I have avoided being subjective in order not to falsify the historical process and the achievements made. I have only recalled the past to help give an account of it, to explain the reasons which stimulated the constant developments and continuous modifications, at the rate required by the circumstances at each specific moment.

The idea of writing a book about the Cooperative Experience is quite an old one, and previous books were published in 1979 and 1984, somewhat hurriedly. These publications satisfactorily fulfilled their purpose of informing about the Experience.

However, in Otalora, the Centre for Cooperative Education and Dissemination, and Management Training, it was thought necessary to give more conceptual and historical information, transforming what was aimed at informing visitors and new members about our Cooperative Experience, into a more up-to-date publication, while dealing with the reasons behind the Experience and looking in more detail at its origins.

To give a more systematic coverage, it was thought that the order of the book should follow the initiatives considered basic in the consolidation of Mondragón cooperativism.

For this reason, the book, after a chapter devoted to the Foundation of the Experience, covers Hezibide, the Educational Group, and Eskola Politeknikoa, a school which was created in 1943 and whose influence, never sufficiently appreciated by the actual protagonists of the experience, has been central in the social model applied to enterprises.

The third chapter deals with Caja Laboral Popular, a Credit Institution whose support in the consolidation of the Group as a whole has been decisive and probably the most significant reason behind the development of the Group into what it is today.

Next comes Lagun-Aro, now a Voluntary Social Welfare Body, whose institutional support in providing Social Security benefits, with strong cooperative roots, differentiates the level of autonomy which the Mondragon Cooperative Group has demonstrated in this respect from its inception, clarifying the cooperative members' status as self-employed workers.

To conclude this process of analysis there is a chapter on the Industrial and Service Group. This is the most well known and strongest aspect of the Experience, owing to its entrepreneurial and social achievements and to the encouraging prospects which are attributed to it. It was also necessary to cover aspects related to the social theses drawn up through the daily management of the Experience, its cooperatives and its members. After all, its distinguishing features, bearing out the social image it has projected, should be stated somewhere. In October 1987, the 1st Congress of the Mondragon Cooperative Group approved the 10 Basic Principles, which are adhered to by all the protagonists of this modest Experience at the service of everyone.

My dear readers, you may be sure that the book that you now hold in your hands was written, just like everything else in the Experience, to help others to participate fully in a common and shared achievement, in which everything revolves around men and women and their work, which in short is their greatest asset.

REMEMBERING DON JOSE MARIA

There is a force which is evident in practically every chapter of this book: it is the message, the influence and the utopianism of the apparently impossible proposals of the founder of the Experience, Don José María Arizmendiarrieta.

He arrived in Mondragón at the beginning of February 1941. The year of the publication of this book, 1991, will witness the 50th anniversary of his arrival. He devoted his first 15 years in Mondragón to youth education, encouraging the young people of the town to look beyond the confines of a town located far from the economic, cultural and political centres of the region.

He lived another twenty years, 1955-1975, completely immersed in the development process of all the most important initiatives: Eskola Politeknikoa, the first cooperative, the first cooperative group, Caja Laboral Popular, Lagun-Aro and Ikerlan.

It would have been difficult to have undertaken everything that the Experience encompasses, in imagination, necessity and success, without his presence as a pillar of ideological support, as a creator of trust and as indisputable leader.

The men who put into practice what he proposed received his ideas as a wave of new concepts, which fell on them still unfashioned, barely developed. It was therefore very difficult to follow him; not only due to the fact that his plans required effort, but because, being just ideas, they were abstract and escaped the pioneers, who were used to handling precise mechanical concepts and basic economic projects.

The cooperators who were taught by him, learnt from the way he lived to accept naturally that all men have equal rights. They also believed in work as the principal means of achieving wellbeing.

Those who came to the Experience later try to explain its roots through a combination of a series of factors, each of which are seen as equally necessary and important.

There is in all probability a flaw in the formulation of this analysis, because the only influence which distinguishes the roots of the Mondragón Experience from any other with the same aspirations at that time, is the presence in Mondragon of Don José María Arizmendiarrieta.

He was an essential agent. In the Basque Country there were many other examples of social initiatives, based on theoretical formulas which did not tackle "structural change" in depth and were not practical. The Basque Country is a small land, with rough, green terrain. Its people take heart from the magical effect of tough yet intimate challenges. They always yearn for change, progress, are non-conformist and unrefined, looking for solutions through a dynamic exchange of unfulfillable aspirations.

But it was here, to Mondragón, that Don José María Arizmendiarrieta came 50 years ago, to promote and channel dissipated forces, which had emerged from the recently concluded Spanish Civil War, before, if chance permitted, they should escape downstream like the rapid and turbid waters of the local steep valley streams.

It is, without doubt, Don José María Arizmendiarrieta's memory, inevitably explicit in every chapter, that has motivated us to set down, in practical language, something about which we feel others should know.

José María Ormaechea
5th February 1991

ULGOR 1958, when the train still went by.

“This Cooperative Experience has resulted in a community alert to and made aware of worries and values which human experience has today taken to heart. It could be said that it is born and fed by a state of new social awareness, whose most notable features could be broken down in the following way:

a) An awareness of freedom, not just formal, but real, that as such, needs to be embodied in socio-economic realities.

b) An awareness of social justice, which first of all induces a new system of solidarity and social order.

c) An awareness of development, with the requirement that potential resources, such as labour and savings, be mobilised.

d) An awareness of participation, which, accepting the need for the organizational ladder, requires control and democratic action to prevent man from being imprisoned by it. (J.Mª Arizmendiarrieta)”

1. THE BIRTH OF THE EXPERIENCE

1.1 EXPERIENCING A NEW TYPE OF ENTERPRISE

Anyone deciding to investigate the origins of the Cooperative Experience will look for its roots in Mondragón. However, it is not easy to give a concise explanation of something for which scholars wish to find a basic reason, encompassing all the ingredients which made it possible.

In the end, when attempting to give an account of the nature of relatively complex events, on the one hand, one resorts to simplification and, on the other, to relate what happened, so that the readers themselves can draw their own conclusions. In any case this book has no historicist intention because it is necessarily obliged to describe, in synthesis and only in part, the steps which led to the moment when it can be said that the *Mondragón Cooperative Experience* began to take shape.

What follows is perhaps one way of explaining what happened.

The Spanish Civil War had just come to an end in 1939 and shortly afterwards, in September of that year, the Apprentice School of

The Apprentice School of the Union Cerrajera in Mondragón.

the Union Cerrajera, a large foundry and metalworking company in Mondragón, was founded. The company's Chairman, Ricardo Oreja, in his speech at the opening ceremony said: *"Workers like doctors or like lawyers, are workers for several hours each day, but they are men all day and for their whole life...It is necessary to educate workers fully if we want to avoid a repetition of the catastrophe we have just suffered"*.

The founders started to study and work in the course which this school began, for twelve students. They enroled separately between 1939 and 1942. The classes were mainly devoted to practical work in the workshop and to technical drawing, which were very important in determining final results. The training was aimed at consolidating the knowledge necessary to acquire a good technical base and to become skilled workers who had also studied mathematics, physics, technology, religion, geography, grammar and some French.

After four years of practical work and study, all the students were assured of jobs in the company.

As for the founders, the initial human basis of the Experience, they started in quite important jobs once they had completed the four years. They were rapidly promoted: three becoming foremen and two design engineers.

The founders of the Experience started work, therefore, in the Union Cerrajera of Mondragón, and it was in the Apprentice School where they took their first steps towards acquiring knowledge and practical experience in enterprise management, mainly in production methods.

José María Arizmendiarrieta arrived in Mondragón a little more than two years after the creation of the Apprentice School. At 26 years of age, he was only about ten or twelve years older than the young apprentices, but the difference in disposition between them was much greater.

He quickly gained everyone's affection. He did new things. He spoke of social justice and the need to reform structures. He shunned the traditional model of establishing social relations, pejoratively known as paternalism. A certain climate of perplexity and fear (the memory of the war was still alive) propitiated religious practice and in Acción Católica (an organisation of the Catholic Church), recently organised by his predecessor Roberto Aguirre, Father Arizmendiarrieta maintained an active life full of ambition and restlessness, to which it was

"It should not therefore be a surprise to anybody that they should take to the words of Don José María, as they called him. But let us concentrate on the small events, which were, in effect, the first stutterings of the Cooperative Experience".

not difficult to attract the young people of Mondragon, whose population, diminished by the Civil War, barely totalled 9,000.

In spite of his youth, his condition as a priest, dressed in his full-length attire, suggested, somewhat unusually for that time, a goodness and feeling of enthusiasm and attracted people to his ideas, which were only superficially understood, even by those closest to him.

In the meantime, due to the start of the Second World War in the summer of 1939, there was, as in all Spain, a shortage of food. The most basic items were scarce: bread, cooking oil, vegetables and meat. The way people dressed was relegated to second place owing to the scant margin left by the "primum vivere".

Don José María Arizmendiarrieta found himself in a situation where the town's young people were being fully trained for work, a situation perhaps best exemplified by the students of Apprentice School of the Union Cerrajera. These young people, full of religious fervour,

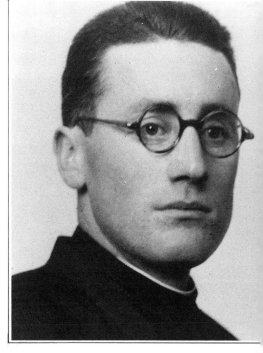

Don José María Arizmendiarrieta. A young priest arrives in Mondragón.

had been born in very humble families in years of social collapse and were on the verge of pathological hunger.

It should not therefore be a surprise to anybody that they should take to the words of Don José María, as they called him. But let us concentrate on the small events, which were, in effect, the first stutterings of the Cooperative Experience.

Don José María said, in October 1943, in the edition of "Aleluya" magazine published to be sent to the young men doing their military service:

"Life is like a perfume or an aroma, once it is gone you can never get it back again. Should I not pay attention to how I spend it? ... Life is for living!, let me tell you elaborating on the words of Ramón y Cajal, life is for living, not according to the impulses of nature, as the stoics and the systematic Rousseau declared, but according to the norms of science and art, which, in short, are also mandates of clarified nature and purified by knowledge of them.

On the eve of Epiphany. Preparing the procession.

Life must be lived according to the dictates of reason and faith, clarifying and perfecting the way which is partially lit by reason. Be men and be christian".

In the summer of the same year, General Franco came to Mondragon, invited as a guest at the wedding of the Count and Countess of Monterron, and the editor (the secretary of Acción Católica) ironically informed about the event not knowing that Franco was present: *"There we were in our dress suits. We kissed a few ladies. We kissed their hands. The reception was very lively. Sixty cars. A good menu. Aristocratic humour. After nine, just like everyday, it started to get dark. Night fell, like it always does. The staff of the magazine are very grateful for the invitation to witness the wedding from "Kondekua" bridge".*

For reasons such as this, "Aleluya" had to change its name to "Equis" (X) and later to "Ecos" (Echoes). These publications appeared in their terminal phase as mural newspapers in the Acción Católica headquarters, finally being torn down by the Civil Guard. These incidents, which perfectly exemplify the situation, occurred when their protagonists were only seventeen years old.

"The fact is that a non-conformist atmosphere progressively grew up around Father Arizmendiarrieta, at the same time that the young people were leading very active lives."

The fact is that a non-conformist atmosphere progressively grew up around Father Arizmendiarrieta, at the same time that the young people were leading very active lives. The football team, which had previously been known as Mondragon F.C., was revived as Juventud Deportiva de Mondragon, a sports club. This club offered a wider range of options for playing some sort of sport and, above all, owned enough land, that later, using some more adjoining land, the **Eskola Politeknikoa** could be built in 1960/65, when the cooperatives created ten years before, could finance it.

Sport took up most of the young peoples' free time.

Theatrical performances, Twelfth Night processions, "Bizar Zuri", (1) "Olentzero" (2) at Christmas, were some of the activities established to keep young people occupied, to prevent them from getting into trouble, if left to their own devices.

This was the situation in the years after the Civil War, when the founders were finishing their studies in mechanics in the Union Cerrajera, whilst working closely on the initiatives of Father Arizmendi. There was a somewhat contradictory situation. The satisfactory

Religious celebrations were a part of daily life.

[1] A white bearded messenger, whose job it was, before Christmas, to collect the letters children wrote to the Three Wise Men asking for the presents they wanted.

[2] A mythical Basque figure, who normally worked in the mountains, doing rough work, and who came down to the town during the winter solstice to announce the New Year.

presence of a priest in the socio-religious class, which he gave on saturday evenings for the students of the School, was upset by the new ideas he presented. His language, not properly constructed syntactically, using uncommon terms, and hard to grasp in terms of harmony, was cryptic and almost soporific. But Father Arizmendi was never one to be discouraged by the better or worse impact which his manner produced, although he was careful in his dress and always very polite. He was neither a great orator nor did he get carried away with lyricism and rhetoric. It took a lot of effort for him to compensate for this deficiency. In the end, we shall have to judge whether his prose, shed of lavishness and embodied by austerity, was not an important part of the message which his followers could not clearly perceive.

The contradiction with the Union Cerrajera occurred because his ideas, translated into the classroom of the Apprentice School, were in the end going to unleash a degree of tension which would finally result in the creation of the cooperatives.

In 1943 Father Arizmendi had created, practically alone, the Escuela Profesional. By 1946, using this platform he proposed that the young men trained in the Union Cerrajera School, who at that time held quite important posts in the company, should undertake higher education in engineering.

By way of collaboration achieved in a very personal manner he convinced Don José Sinues y Urbiola, Director of the Engineering School in Zaragoza and President of the Confederation of Spanish Savings Banks, that these students did not have to attend class in Zaragoza. The school created by Father Arizmendi would provide the necessary training in Mondragón for students to pass, year after year, courses in mechanics, chemistry and electricity, without abandoning their jobs; in other words, combining work with study.

Eleven students sat the entry exam in 1946 and completed their final projects in 1952.

It was now time to initiate new proposals based progressively on an uninterrupted social maturity.

Between 1949 and 1950 there was social turmoil in the heart of the Union Cerrajera. The company, weighed down by an excessive number of workers off sick, decided to modify the corresponding benefit in such a way that..."*workers with an average salary of 30 to 35 pesetas a day would have their wage reduced to 10 to 14 pesetas, less than 30% of their real wages.*

The intention of the company was to impose forcefully, with violence, a criteria which was not ours and that we did not accept because it was wrong".

The studies, analyses, trips, meetings and discrepancies of the founders of the cooperatives, produced something unusual. As the men in charge of the workshops, with many workers under their charge, they publicly opposed the decisions of top management and the Board. Moreover, when the workers "illegally" went out on strike, the foremen and engineers to whom Father Arizmendi had been directing his message, did so as well.

It was no surprise, therefore, when around Christmas 1950 the Managing Director of the Union Cerrajera called two of his foremen (later significant cooperators) to his office to tell them that they should stop stirring up the workers because *"apostles should practise in India, not in my factory. The men I need have to learn to change their opinions when I ask them to".* He hoped that they would change their ideas in two weeks and confident that they would he then called them in again, but the required brainwashing had not taken place.

An unforgettable sight. Don José María and his bicycle.

On 23rd February 1954 the whole workforce voted to elect the members of the "jurado de empresa" (a consultative body created as a substitute for collective bargaining) and, with the elections won, the Sindicato Vertical del Metal (metalworkers' union) accredited two of the future cooperators. The meetings chaired by the management of the company were animated. Many years had gone by since the establishment of the Franco dictatorship. The conduct of the power in the land had been subliminally transmitted to all spheres of society. Company bosses, unfearing of the Sindicato Vertical, did not want to share decision making.

These men did not conclude their term (1954 to 1957) on the "jurado". In the short time that they lasted they requested, amongst other things, social improvements, the establishment of the so-called English saturday (half-day working) for the shopfloor workers (office staff already enjoyed it) and the distribution of part of an increase in capital which was going to be carried out at that time, amongst the workers.

The calculations made to finance the English saturday early in 1955 showed that it would cost 650,000 pesetas, about 22 to 25 million pesetas in current pesetas, of the total payroll. At that time labour costs accounted for between 6 to 8% of turnover, with an average wage of 45 pesetas a day (18,000 pesetas a year), including two extra payments in July and December. So it can be deduced that the cost of salaries was going to increase by about 3%

As far as the increase in capital was concerned, the proposal for which was to distribute 20% as workers' shares, the argument was that *"increases in capital were an inalienable right of the shareholders"*.

What with studying, work and some social skirmishes, the days and years prior to the creation of the first cooperative company were lived intensely and fully.

What had been proved was that in-depth company reform from within was impossible. The law which could not be broken, the pleasant and impenetrable monotony of a paternalistic legislation, contributed to the maintenance of company structures in which the "worker shall be the son of a worker" and the "engineer the son of the engineer". The abundant results, in a strongly autarchic economy, were the indisputable heritage of those who contributed capital and, at that time, very little effort.

In the meantime the Study Circles in Acción Católica and in JOC (Young Catholic Workers Movement) continued at progressively higher levels. During the summer, under the aegis of the Diocesan Secretariat in Vitoria, Father Arizmendi organised specialist courses on sociology to which he invited economics professors such as Paris Eguilaz and Velarde Fuertes. His ecclesiastical training led him towards being a practical apostle. He not only tried to give guidelines on what should be the model for the ideal enterprise, an intellectual inhibition to which theorists are very devoted, but he also put that social enterprise to which he aspired into practice. *"We ourselves will have to reform companies internally giving maximum consideration to the freedom and personality of the workers. It falls to us to make a start, by renouncing some of the privileges which we have"*.

In 1954 a timid start was made on a study for the embryo of an enterprise with the name of ASTEC (Asesoramientos Tecnicos (Technical Consultations)) which just about completed a project for a gantry crane.

In the same year a malleable cast iron foundry was planned, the study for which Father Arizmendi lucidly, although with excessive hopefulness, presented in the Caja de Ahorros Provincial (Provincial Savings Bank), where it plunged into anonymity.

on tape

U satorre, Luis

L arrañaga, Jesús

ULGOR

**The five
founders
of the
Experience
in 1956.**

G orroñogoitia, Alfonso

O rmaechea, José María

o R tubay, Javier

→ '79- Head of Universitates M.

But the idea of creating an enterprise had taken root, and a decision had to be made about how to go about it. There were many unknown factors. Is it the same to venture criteria for reforming companies as to actually apply them? How do you create a company? What are the challenges of the market?; because those who wanted to create their own enterprise had barely mastered production techniques.

But a company is something more. It is a matter of combining intentions, creating an internal organic framework which will work and which is agile. Moreover, it is a matter of going out into a competitive world, already filled by others with their products and services, doing it better and cheaper and, of course, earning money. Then a decision had to be made about how to distribute the profits, a right about which everyone had good ideas and new formulas.

1955 came in a period of industrial restrictions. Electricity was supplied by area and at different times and work was normally in shifts. It was very difficult to get a licence to set up a company. The DOEIS was the State institution responsible for "rationing" the scarce amount of steel produced by the only supplier that there was: Altos Hornos de Vizcaya. The black market was the norm; normal prices and supply were the exception.

The most feasible way of setting up a company was to acquire a licence from an industrialist, which, by transferring the name of the holder, would permit a new company to be set up.

This possibility arose in Vitoria. An aging industrialist, put an advert in the newspaper announcing the sale of his entire business devoted to the production of oil stoves, although it was also licensed to produce "domestic appliances". He was from Aretxabaleta, a town neighbouring Mondragón, and had mastered the craft of metal spinning, which he personally used to manufacture the tanks of the stoves in brass. Otherwise, these stoves had one or two burners, were made of ordinary cast iron and then nickel plated.

On 20th October 1955 the transfer contract was signed for the premises in Calle Comandante Izarduy No. 5, Vitoria, and Luis Usatorre went there immediately to "watch the shop", which had been purchased for 400,000 pesetas. The others followed throughout 1956.

Of the eleven apprentices, five had been chosen. Later another three or four would come aboard in new cooperatives. This design owed much to chance, to the subliminal message of Father Arizmendi, to the decision of those best situated in the Union Cerrajera or, as is more likely, to a combination of all these factors to a greater or lesser extent.

But a start had been made. On 14th April 1956 a 750 m^2 two storey concrete structure was erected on a plot of land known as "Laxarte" in Mondragón. On 12th November that same year, the company headquarters was moved there from Vitoria, with some urgency.

The company adopted the name "Talleres Ulgor". This name being the acrostic formed by the initial letters of the surnames of the five founders of the "Experience".

The cooperative structure, grounded on previously accepted ideological bases, came later, after studying other options amongst the different enterprise models which could have been legally adopted.

It was not until March 1959 that the first company statutes of "Talleres Ulgor, S.C.I." (Industrial Cooperative Society) were approved, once that the cooperative system had been found to be the best system available, at that time, to break with the attitudes deeply rooted in traditional ideas.

The break with the traditional way of managing an enterprise had been made. Looking at the situation from all sides it was not easy to make this break without taking time to reflect a little.

The company which had trained the founders was in the hands of managers and directors who were active practising catholics and, as a result, profoundly concerned about social issues. Under the management system in force a lot of attention had been given to the training of apprentices, in showing them all types of industrial experiences and in the wide range of technical options which the Union Cerrajera of Mondragón displayed through the scope of its business activities.

Rafael Amozarrain

José Ayala

Félix González

Jesús Letona

Pioneers of the Experience.

It was a pioneering company in its social programmes: the Hermandad de Trabajadores (Workers Brotherhood) to cover complementary social contingencies, a forerunner of Social Security, the Apprentice School and its Library, the sports area, economic housing for its employees, the subsidised company shop (Economato), refresher courses for adults, the Antituberculosis Clinic created to protect against and control the endemic spread of this disease, due to the hunger people were suffering; not to mention the onerous support given to make it easier to attend spiritual retreats, which practically all the staff did, the collaboration in all social, cultural activities, etc. All these activities indisputably made the company the magnanimous and exemplary entity of the moment due to its appreciable, protective and charitable contribution.

However the charitable nature of these implicit bonuses received by the workers in these round-about ways showed how outmoded they were.

At the same time the company, protected by impervious customs duties, was obtaining excellent results. This led to the mistaken belief that what was in reality the product of political, union, commercial and economic protectionism, was due to impeccable management.

This was not so. That is to say, advantage was not taken of the circumstances to make capital investments and to update the range of products, nor to retrain the large workforce which needed to be prepared for the more hostile times to come.

Life went on in a paternalist atmosphere moulded by the authoritarian and protective regime which had its origin in the State, whose influence extended vertically throughout society. Because the situation was reproduced in a similar fashion in all the country's industries.

 *n 20th October 1955 the transfer contract was signed for the premises in Calle Comandante Izarduy No. 5, Vitoria, and Luis Usatorre went there immediately to "watch the shop", which had been purchased for 400,000 pesetas. The others followed throughout 1956."*

For this reason the break with and departure from Union Cerrajera of those who were to become cooperators did not create significant tensions and, perhaps, although lamenting the fact - *"I cannot deny the pain it has caused me"* wrote the Managing Director of Union Cerrajera on 3rd April 1956 to one of the future cooperators - their departure was a release and the end of a process whose origins lay in the need to undertake the structural change suggested by Don José Mariá Arizmendiarrieta ten years before. The short history of industry in the Basque Country has made it clear that the predictions were not unfounded and that renovation was necessary, from the point of view of both social balance and technological rearmament.

In 1990 the following balance can be drawn: the Union Cerrajera of Mondragón, which in 1955 had 1,350 workers, now has 270 in Mondragón; whilst the cooperative workers in Mondragón exceed 5,000, forming part of a census of more than 22,000 jobs in the Basque Country as a whole, when in 1956 there were only 16. What would have become of this town and the Alto

The FAGOR "Maite" stove.

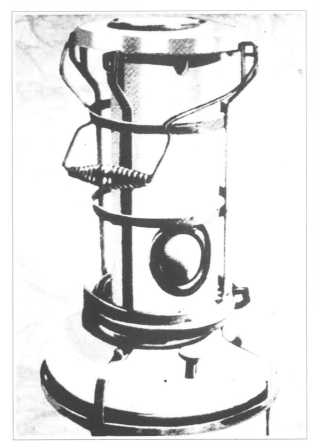

The FAGOR "Dorothy" heater.

Deba area, which has 9,000 workers in the cooperatives, if the Experience had not been so timely in its appearance?

However it would not be correct to leave the analysis of the **first steps of cooperativism here at this point.**

The start of social change, back then at the start of 1941 when Don José María arrived in Mondragón, is the most distant milestone and where the first steps can be seen. The flow of contributions from other sources started above all from 1962, seven years after the start of Ulgor. It came from men who were greatly concerned and who were, in all probability, guided by similar reasons in pursuit of company reform.

Basically the initial vocation was enriched by such men who brought their professionalism and helped consolidate the Experience with new ideas. From the start the idea was to restrict the cooperatives to the Basque Country, not for strictly political reasons, and at all events nothing to do with taking a categorically exclusive stance, but due rather to the fact that the capacity for action could not extend beyond the boundaries where control was profoundly human - and therefore its proximity was necessary - and carried out in an environment in which the process for structural change was understood as a necessary spiritual value to which to aspire.

no longer a necessity — w/ web?

In an effort to synthesize, which always implies the risk of leaving some options out, it could be said that the Experience added the following ideological vehicles to its markedly social emphasis:

"T*he start of social change, back then at the start of 1941 when Don José María arrived in Mondragón, is the most distant milestone and where the first steps can be seen. The flow of contributions from other sources started above all from 1962, seven years after the start of Ulgor.*"

a) The commitment to the Basque Country, clearly evident from 1970: *"every effort shall be made to strengthen economically the country it serves to which end it shall promote enterprise development through expansion and respond to its permanent vocation towards human freedom."*

1962. The inauguration of FAGOR ELECTRONICA

b) The new professionals who came out of the Eskola Politeknikoa, whose influence was to be decisive, above all in the creation of new cooperatives and in taking over in time, from the original founders.

c) The contribution of members with trade union credentials within the cooperative order. They have been capable of keeping top management

1965. The awarding of the Gold Medal for Work; the first official recognition.

in the cooperatives aware of the habitual concerns of the rank-and-file members, less inclined to understand and interpret the key needs of the company, but more so with immediate and unavoidable needs.

d) The contribution of diverse origin from universities or the social world, with a desire to break the status quo, following a firm and strong ethically conceived path in the organisation of work and the distribution of company profits.

However, there can be no doubt that the basic social source had its origins in Mondragon. It was something that for almost fifteen years Father Arizmendiarrieta was preparing in an almost imperceptible way for those who were later to be the main protagonists driven by him.

He found a society defenceless after the turmoil of a devastating civil war, in a climate halted by a fear of breaking an imposed sense of balance, in a context of absolute physical need, with a youth which could be driven by any popular cause capable of creating the least illusion and hope.

Any one of the components of this singular situation was necessary, and between them all they made it possible. The conclusion can equally be reached that if any one of these conditions had been wanting, the Experience would never have crystallised.

The School goes on, Don José María's message remains.

"The sense of present history teaches us that to survive and develop, apart from rationalising production and being competitive in the market place, all companies have to strengthen their workforce; and even more so, if the enterprise was founded with a cooperative spirit, that is to say, as an instrument of the popular classes in our country for their collective development; not so much from an economic point of view, the essential base to enable us to aspire to greater improvement, but from an overrall view, of being human, free, aware and "dealienated". (J. Mª Arizmendiarrieta)".

* 2. HEZIBIDE, EDUCATIONAL GROUP
ESKOLA POLITEKNIKOA

"Give a man a fish and he will have food
for a day; teach him to fish and he will
have food for the rest of his life".
(Chinese proverb)

2.1. A BRIEF HISTORY

1941: Don José María Arizmendiarrieta arrives in Mondragón

It was on the 5th February that Don José María Arizmendiarrieta, a newly ordained priest, arrived in Mondragón as coadjutor to the Parish of San Juan Bautista.

These were difficult times; the civil war had left the town divided and in ruins, economically speaking. Pacifist rhetoric was superfluous and there was an urgent need for social justice, for an opening up towards new ideas of participation and social integration.

Don José María took his first steps in the educational field in the Apprentice School of the Union Cerrajera. He soon realised that the school was not sufficient to feed the desire to get on in the youth of Mondragón, as there was a reduced quota for admission of 10 to 12 students per year.

1943: Opening of the Escuela Profesional

Thanks to the support of the Parents Association of Acción Católica, a Board of Governors was constituted in order to create a Technical College.

In order to make the project viable, the building of the Escuela de Viteri, a charitable educational foundation, was used as it was available at that time.

So once they had a building and a studies programme for Elementary Technical Colleges for a cycle of four courses, suitable teachers were contracted and a private loan was obtained to purchase furniture and machinery .

The help of all the companies in the area was requested for upkeep, by means of a lump sum per worker per year. Likewise, the members of the Association imposed a monthly quota to that end.

With this help the **Escuela Profesiona**l was inaugurated on 10th October 1943, with 20 students registered.

---

* This chapter was written by Juan Leibar.

Among the Board of Governors, made up of all the "main forces" in the town, conservative attitudes came to the fore, in the belief that it was a risk to permit access to so many aspirants, who at the end of their vocational training, with a higher cultural and technical level could be the source of revolutionary ferment in local companies.

The tenet that "the son of an engineer shall be an engineer and the son of a worker, a worker" was about to be broken, or there was at least the danger of it.

1947: The First Graduates

A very important step was taken in promoting local youth: the Technical Engineering School in Zaragoza authorised the students of the Escuela Professional in Mondragón to study in absentia, after an attempt was made to get the same support in Bilbao.

Don José María Arizmendiarrieta encouraged a group of young men whose aspirations were not satisfied with elementary technical education. They wanted something more. Twelve students undertook to take higher level technical studies in absentia, overcoming all the difficulties that this supposed.

After five academic years of redoubled effort, they completed their studies and graduated, nine in Mechanics, another in Electricity and two in Chemistry.

From this first batch, the founders of Ulgor, the first industrial cooperative in Mondragon, would later emerge in 1955: Usatorre, Larrañaga, Gorroñogoitia, Ormaechea and Ortubay.

1948: The League of Education and Culture

At a meeting of the "main forces" in Mondragon, the Charter of an Association called the League of Education and Culture was approved, to provide a legal means of channelling the collaboration of various local public and private bodies, from municipal ones to union ones, from entrepreneurs to workers ...

There were about one hundred students who alternated work with study: 6 hours in the classroom and doing practical work in the School's workshop and 4 hours paid work in a factory.

1952: A new building and more space

A second phase began: With the help of the Minister for Education, Mr Ruiz Gimenez, the new Escuela Profesional was inaugurated in the enormous Cometal building (now the local hospital).

The 150 students were lost in that iron and concrete structure (4 stories each measuring 850 m^2 on a plot of 2,000 m^2) with a capacity for 1,000 students. Some people accused Don

José María of being mad, for getting involved in such economic and social ventures.

1957: Vocational Training comes of age

A key year for vocational education.

With Guillermo Reyna as Director General of Vocational Education, Vocational Training was profoundly reformed, with these studies forming part of state education, recognised alongside other types of study. The responsibility for Vocational Training passed from the Ministry of Work to the Ministry of Education and Science.

The new formula was immediately introduced in the Escuela Profesional: three years of Oficialia Industrial and two more to complete Maestria Industrial, in the branches of Mechanics and Electricity. The special subject of radio engineering was incorporated, forming the basis of what would subsequently become the Electronics branch.

The School even went as far as to set up its own radio station, known as the Parish Radio station. In other words it had religious backing, because otherwise it was impossible to receive official permission for this sort of communications media.

In 1958 the first class of students began their studies in Industrial Draughtsmanship. Opening up new horizons, Chemistry was introduced as a special subject, aimed mainly at female students.

A group of students with their teachers.

Filing was an essential subject.

Around that time Don José María wrote: *"It is a great error that girls do not generally have access to Vocational Education and, of course, do not also participate in all processes of reconversion and in-service training, giving them entry to professions which today are denied them because they are unsuitable ..."*.

1960: The glorious decade

The sixties was a prolific period for the cooperative movement initiated by Don José María:

- **Caja Laboral Popular** was already in existence; **Lagun-Aro** started life under its wing.

- The groundwork was done for the Health Centre (today the local hospital for the Alto Deba area) with the backing of the **League of Welfare and Education.**

- The League of Education and Culture became a *"cooperative dedicated to educational activities"*, thus legally forming part of the **Mondragón Cooperative Experience**, for which it has been the cradle.

- The cooperatives were consolidated by means of rapid expansion, especially in the Alto Deba. The following cooperatives were formed **Ulgor, Arrasate, Copreci, Fagor-Electronica, Ederlan, Eroski ...**

- The Escuela Profesional exceeded all the forecasts made; more than 1,000 students registered in academic year 1963-64. **In 1965 the Escuela Profesional Politecnica** and the sports complex were inaugurated in Iturripe, on a plot of over 40,000 m2.

- In 1976 a new cooperative was formed, which was unique in its type: **Alecop** (the student cooperative), a company managed by the students of the Escuela Profesional, with the collaboration of some teachers or ex-students as monitors.

"By means of this organisation a valuable scholastic protection for students was automatically generated; they were taught social management and initiative; it helped students to work and workers to study ...".

Another very important date in the history of the Escuela Profesional Politecnica was 1968: After the visit of the Minister of Education, Lora Tamayo, the school was **officially recognised as a University School for Technical Engineering**, authorised not only to impart these studies, but also to award the corresponding qualifications.

This was the culmination of the recognition cycle. It was a significant step towards the aim of *"socialising knowledge in order to democratise power"*, with the practical and progressive application of equal opportunities. The school had come of age.

Another of the initiatives created in this decade was the **Mondragon Language School (Ahizke-CIM)**, which later broke away from the School to set up in its own right.

In front of the school. A memory to treasure.

Iraunkor (In-service Training Department) and **Ikerlan** (Research and Development Centre) were also created at this time.

Finally:

The seventies and eighties have not yet come to form part of history, they are still there, in sight, within reach. A brief glance will show what has been going on with regard to this technical and cultural institution which we know as the Eskola Politeknikoa.

"*The new formula was immediately introduced in the Escuela Profesional: three years of Oficialia Industrial and two more to complete Maestria Industrial, in the branches of Mechanics and Electricity. The special subject of radio engineering was incorporated, forming the basis of what would subsequently become the Electronics branch.*"

2.2 THE EDUCATIONAL GROUP TODAY

The association known as the League of Education and Culture has today been transformed into **Hezibide, Educational Group**, whose *"purpose is to plan, coordinate and promote educational activities in the Alto Deba area, by means of the combined participation of the associated Educational Centres ...".*

This coordination, planning and promotion covers three private University Schools in the Alto Deba area; the University School for Technical Engineering in Mondragón, the Business Studies College in Oñati and the Teacher Training College in Eskoriatza, in addition to the School-leaving Examination and Vocational Training Centres in the Eskola Politeknikoa, the colleges of San Viator and Almen ... Basque schools, nursery schools and kindergartens ... not forgetting Ahizke-Cim, the language school.

More than 6,000 students study within the state education system in these schools and colleges, that is to say, not taking into account the students of Ahizke and Iraunkor.

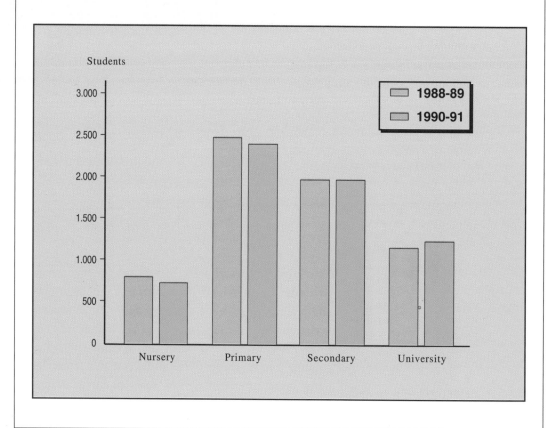

Gizabidea

The **Gizabidea Foundation** was a posthumous creation of Don José María Arizmendiarrieta, its *"aim is to promote, on a non- profit making basis, education and, especially, research and technological and social training for a progressive socio-economic transformation ...".*

Hezibide and Gizabidea work side by side to make the best economic resources of the Alto Deba in the educational and research centres.

Eskola Politeknikoa

In this Educational Group, the **Eskola Politeknikoa** and its achievements are worthy of special attention.

Today, **José María Arizmendiarrieta Eskola Politeknikoa** (for that is its official name, in honour of its founder) has more than 2,000 students, of which half are studying Engineering.

Partial view of Eskola Politeknikoa today.

But, apart from state education, Eskola Politeknikoa has developed other initiatives which are now fertile fields.

Alecop

From the start, the students of Eskola have combined their studies with work in an industrial enterprise. In 1976 an original cooperative was created, made up of college students, students of Vocational Education and Engineering: **Alecop.**

Today it has 600 members who exercise self-management, who are students from Eskola Politeknikoa, Irakasle Eskola (the Teacher Training College) and ETEO (the Business Studies College).

Alecop has the following aims as far as social advancement is concerned:

-To self-finance the studies and living expenses of the students.

-To offer real work experience.

A group of students, hard at work.

-To complete the studies and practical work offered by the School.

-To give training in social participation and enterprise management.

Alecop is a fully fledged company, with its own production, and a service of lending out labour to other companies.

Ahizke-Cim

From the modest premises of Eskola the language school has moved to new premises occupying 2.000 m², becoming an Educational Cooperative linked to Hezibide.

It gives classes in English, French, German and Italian to children, adults and companies. More than 2,000 students register annually.

We should now take a brief look at other projects, based in Eskola Politeknikoa, which although not forming part of the state education system, provide support for it.

Saiolan: Innovation and business development

Saiolan is a centre for training promoters and developing new business activities.

Its promotion work is carried out by means of training programmes and preparing potential promoters in the development of a project, involving a product, process or service for which all the technological-business aspects are analyzed.

Some projects are of a generic nature, financed in general, by public funds; others are more specific, financed and taken on by the companies which commission them.

The Monitor Group, formed by highly experienced professional experts, and the teams of postgraduate scholarship holders work in areas of preferential interest: making various production processes more flexible, new manufacturing technologies, food technology and science, biotechnology, new materials, services for the quality of life and active leisure, etc.

Iraunkor

The Eskola Politeknikoa of Mondragon and ETEO (Business Studies College) of Oñati have set themselves the goal of offering industry, in an integral fashion, either directly or by subcontrating, all sorts of courses which meet the training needs felt by companies. It is, in short, an in- service training centre.

New educational equipment in Eskola.

Today **Iraunkor** offers courses in the following specific fields: technology, production, marketing, administration-finance, management. In the academic year 1989-90, more than 5,000 class hours were given.

Relations have been consolidated with various Spanish institutions dedicated to the in-service training of postgraduates and managers, in order to prepare programmes and teaching staff for the Production Management and Systems Engineering masters degree courses, envisaged in the Long Term Plan.

Goier

Its purpose is to make it viable for Technical Engineering graduates, who have demonstrated that they have the right disposition and attitude, to study abroad.

Today more than fifty students from Eskola Politeknikoa are completing their studies, to obtain masters degrees or doctorates at polytechnics or universities in France, Great Britain, Belgium, Italy, Switzerland, United States

Finally

Hezibide and the Educational Group have made their own Don José María Arizmendiarrieta's maxim that: *"The sign of vitality is not to perdure, but to be reborn and to adapt"*.

"*C*aja Laboral Popular tries to develop the community directly and the individual through the community. For this reason it transforms its resources into community loans, which as such are intended for legally established cooperatives, and through them for their members. By means of this procedure it tries to protect, as far as possible, the social function of property and economic wealth, by establishing its main objective as the development of the community and of people through the community. In this way, individual and community wealth, public and private property are intimately synchronised. (J. Mª Arizmendiarrieta)".*

3. CAJA LABORAL POPULAR

Together with the Escuela Profesional Politecnica, Caja Laboral Popular was the most important institution created by Don José María Arizmendiarrieta.

It is said that big businessmen should make long term plans and anticipate events in time so as to be able to overcome setbacks effectively when they occur.

Training as an indispensable means of carrying out a work of a popular, economic and social foundation, starting from the unlimited resources of personal effort, had to be accompanied by accumulated work, by the savings of other generations and by other segments of society not necessarily involved in the Cooperative Experience which had already sprouted forth. The difficulty lay not so much in the technicalities of starting up the finance company conceived by Arizmendiarrieta, but in his having to do everything in his power, yet again, to convince the indispensable protagonists to accept the idea warmly and without reservations.

Today it is difficult to imagine the **Mondragon Cooperative Group without Caja Laboral Popular**. The passing of more than thirty years has shown that the predictions were well founded and that without its financial cooperation it would have been

The Mondragón branch in Calle Iturriotz, after refurbishment. Caja Laboral Popular started life here.

impossible to have developed the social experience which the Mondragon Cooperative Group embodies.

3.1 "COOPERATIVISING" MONEY

But four years had gone by since the first industrial initiative was started up in Vitoria under the name **Talleres Ulgor**, and scarcely three since the transfer along with the plant, machinery, products, raw materials and components, to continue developing the chosen activity in the field of domestic appliances. It was early 1959 when Father Arizmendiarrieta began to convince the founders of the Experience of the need to create a credit cooperative.

Accustomed to purchasing land, putting up buildings, designing new products and putting them on the market, financial concepts, distant from the subjects they had studied and from their professional experience, were too abstract for the founders. So a spontaneous rejection, a mixture of impotence and a lack of confidence, was the natural result of the sessions in which Don José María, the real founder of Caja Laboral Popular introduced the idea.

The economic results achieved by the cooperative enterprises were spectacular and this was another deterrent to the insistence on creating a source of greater finance: With 20% of the profits, at the end of the year, the equivalent of 80% of the advance payments (wages) which members had enjoyed over the year could be reinvested.

Given the magnificent response of the domestic market - no thought had yet been given to developing the overseas market - to the products manufactured by the cooperatives, the idea of dedicating time to a project founded on immaterial, or at least professionally inaccessible bases, was almost disturbing.

The economic situation was one of expansion, although the budgetary deficit of the State and the imbalance in the Balance of Payments were deeply rooted, adverse phenomena in the Spanish economy.

At the start of 1957 the Minister of Commerce, Alberto Ullastres and the Treasury Minister, Mariano Navarro attempted to implement a policy of stabilisation.

They tried to gain the support of international bodies such as the International Monetary Fund and the OECD, to which they sent a Memorandum in which they described the taxation and monetary measures which they thought indispensable to contain demand, stabilise prices and reduce import pressure.As a result, at the end of July 1959 Spain joined the OECD having promised to implement measures to liberalise foreign trade, even though the parity of our currency was set at 60 pesetas to the dollar.

A certain breath of fresh air, based on opportunist currents, was felt in the atmosphere. However, the restriction on credit imposed by the Bank of Spain and the problems with banks in general put large sectors of the Basque economy in serious difficulties. Amongst these sectors was the machine- tool sector, based principally in and around Elgoibar. Ullastres, the Minister of Commerce, visited the town to get an idea at close hand of the consequences of his measures for stabilisation, the first measures which enabled an escape from the iron grip of autarky, in which companies had found themselves during more than twenty years of dictatorship.

This situation meant that Caja Laboral Popular was surreptitiously born in a preliminary phase which began in Mondragon on 15th March, 1959.

There are minutes to a meeting that was never actually held, in which the following was agreed:

1. To form a Credit Cooperative whose Statutes have been approved

2. To appoint a provisional Governing Council

3. To appoint a Supervisory Board (Auditors)

Once the procedures were completed in rigorous respect of the

Zumárraga branch.

norms, the Company Statutes were approved on 16th July, 1959 and on 28th of the same month authorization was given by the Ministry of Work, which at that time had almost exclusive responsibility for registering, regulating and inspecting Credit Cooperatives.

On 24th December of the same year **Caja Laboral Popular** was definitively formed, **founded by Ulgor, Funcor, Arrasate and the San José Consumer Cooperative**. The meeting was held in the headquarters of Ulgor. The Caja was faced with a tremendous task which it had to undertake without delay, in that through its Social Section it had to immediately begin to cover essential sickness benefits because, as we shall see in the next chapter, that same year members of industrial cooperatives had been excluded from the Spanish Social Security System.

With the creation of Caja Laboral Popular, by its own definition and authorised activities, there now existed an instrument whose role was to act as intermediary in attracting resources, to administer them and to use them for community development through cooperativism.

Whereas the industrial cooperatives had managed to cooperativise work, as had the consumer cooperatives at the same time - the latter being more familiar, with roots dating back to the start of the century -, the cooperativisation of money was not easy to assimilate and difficult to reduce to understandable terms. But like all activities as they become established, the idea of credit took on a more familiar face and, progressively, the objectives, applications and the model for the relationship between the cooperatives, the ultimate beneficiaries, and Caja Laboral Popular were determined.

3.2. THE FIRST STEPS: FROM 1960 TO 1970

The first branch office was opened early in 1960 in Calle Ferrerías 40 in Mondragón and that same year it moved to Calle José Mª Resusta 27 - now Calle Iturriotz 31 - to the building which had been constructed for the San José Consumer Cooperative, from which Caja Laboral Popular purchased it.

At first, the volume of deposits to be handled was small. At the end of its first year in 1960, credit balance totalled 6,452,355 pesetas, of which 2,825,935 pesetas (43.8%) corresponded to the reserves of the Social Welfare Service, now Lagun-Aro, which advantageously served to finance the group of cooperatives associated with Caja Laboral Popular.

It was not the right time to get people to understand the objective need to create a finance company, bearing in mind the number of such companies already in existence in the Basque Country: the eight very well known and prestigious Savings Banks, the two big Banks in the province of Vizcaya, the Banco Guipuzcoano and Banco de San Sebastian in the province of Guipuzcoa and the Banco de Vitoria in the province of Alava.

On the other hand, never in the proposal for a new cooperative, except at the start when Ulgor and Arrasate were created, had there been any financial anxiety which might make the projects impossible. The stabilisation plan, which had a strong deterrent effect on companies close to the cooperative scene, did not have the slightest effect on the uninterrupted progress of the creation process of new cooperatives and new jobs.

But new ideas arose in the form of stimulating statements, the content of which were, little by little, explained and realized.

"It was necessary (in 1959) to prepare industry, for future and early entry into the Common Market", as well as "to create new companies in the area and region, to absorb demographic growth and avoid the emigration of people from the area". The effort required consisted of: "greater savings, greater capitalization, channelling future increases in savings to making new production investments which would enable the modernisation of industrial plant and the development of new industries, to offer sufficient options for work for the people in the region".

The definitive argument remained forever engraved in the slogan **"Open a savings account, or pack your bags"**. The proposal, in its lyrical bareness, was contaminative, bold and difficult to understand and none the less it was premonitory. At that time unemployment in the Basque Country had scarcely reached 2%, but 26 years later it was nearly 24%; the 20,000 unemployed in 1960 had become about 228,000 in 1986. The strongest industries, whose establishment seemed unshakeable, began to feel the insufficiency of their production equipment and the relentless burden of their lack of innovation. The oil crises of 1973 and 1979 meant that almost all the large companies in the Basque Country suffered from the delaying and accommodating inertia of an artificial economy, created under the protection of a dictatorship, by then over, and isolated from the vigorous reaction of countries which had, however, participated in the Second World War.

In 1961 the following role was advocated for Caja Laboral Popular: *"The level of responsibility is that of high management, compatible at all times with the maximum executive and personalised autonomy of each of the working units. This management requires ample economic and industrial foresight, for which information and constant contact with economic research and planning centres is necessary"*. (Business Plan for 1962. Future direction of Caja Laboral Popular).

Arenal, Bilbao, the Regional Office for Vizcaya.

Under these premises the Group, created around its financial institution, continued to grow rapidly, and only six years later, in 1966, the figures were as follows:

"With the creation of Caja Laboral Popular, by its own definition and authorised activities, there now existed an instrument whose role was to act as intermediary in attracting resources, to administer them and to use them for community development through cooperativism."

	in millions of pesetas -
Sales of the Associated Group	**2,892**
Exports	**(insignificant)**
Personnel	**4,866**
Profit	
(9% over sales, once fixed dividends had been deducted)	258
Credit Balance in CLP	**600**
Total Liabilities CLP	**743**
Capital + Reserves CLP	
(without accumulating profit for the year)	61
Capital Adequacy Ratio	
(without accumulating profit for the year)	**10.2%**
Net profits of CLP for the year	**7.8**

Notice that in spite of seven years having gone by since the creation of CLP, the Associated Group predominated over the financial institution. The total resources of Caja Laboral Popular barely totalled 26% of the sales achieved by the Group. However, it was necessary to have faith in the financial institution and the Associated Group kept that faith.

The formulas of cooperation applied enabled the maintenance of an entity unable to give loans other than to associated cooperatives, by legal definition and by an internal policy decision. However, between 1964 and 1989 the average annual rate of growth of the resources of the Caja was 37% and that for sales of the Group 26%, implying in the space of 25 years a substantial change in the capacity of the Caja to finance the Group easily.

The support that the Group gave to Caja Laboral Popular was essentially as follows:

a) To proceed with its constitution.

b) To contribute continually the capital necessary to maintain correctly the amount of capital plus reserves over the credit resources which affected its solvency.

c) To part with the most important managers of the Group to manage Caja Laboral Popular in its Social Services (Lagun-Aro), Industrial Services (Business Division) and Savings (Banking Division).

d) All the cooperatives terminated their economic- financial activities with other banking institutions, to work only with CLP, even though the services were precarious and, more importantly, that there were insufficient resources to ensure that all lending operations - credits, loans, commercial discount and guarantees - were borne by Caja Laboral.

Dato, Vitoria, the Regional Office for Alava.

This agreement reflected, in its boldness, the trust placed in Caja Laboral Popular by its associated cooperatives. The minutes of the Governing Council meeting held on 29th January 1964 state as follows:

• *AGREEMENT: It is evident that Caja Laboral should be conceived and run on standard business lines, eliminating, at least internally, all the structural obstacles which run counter to the dynamics required by the aforementioned conception. Consequently, the operational policy of the Caja shall be guided by the following principles:*

• *Caja Laboral should become the instrument to polarise and formalise the cooperation of the masses in the economic emancipation of our people. In its operations Caja Laboral should consider itself a separate entity and act in its own right, adapting its technical criteria for expansion to this situation. Thus the function of the Caja "as a bank" is to work with any base cooperative entity, intervening in this activity and risk with operative economic criteria.*

• *Caja Laboral shall try to keep up to date the collective associative processes necessary as they are integrated in a competitive economy, and shall try to direct these by means of various formulas, from the creation of horizontally structured complexes, to the creation of those of the vertically structured second and third degree type.*

• *Caja Laboral shall take care that its regional nature as an institution is equally so in its organisation and scope, to which end, amongst other things, the strongly and profoundly economic criteria in its administration shall be strengthened, due both to the mobility of savings and credit in a cooperative spirit and to the utmost consideration which we owe the sector of the population which has deposited its resources.*

• *It is understood that fully associated cooperatives should consider Caja Laboral as their only bank. This is a presupposition which is considered necessary and an agreement not subject to debate nor reached purely on the basis of goodwill, but technically required in light of the structural function of the Caja with respect to these cooperatives. For reasons of equilibrium it is desirable to try to ensure that the participation of each associate member in the Caja is not greater than 25% of the overall total.*

• *It is essential that an agile and dynamic mechanism be developed for attracting liabilities, particularly those derived from popular savings which represent our main source of resources, to which end the most efficient technological and psychological means shall be used. Caja Laboral should actively pay attention to the advance preparation of infrastructural elements to guarantee or develop new industrial or social companies. In this respect*

"*The model of a return on savings with the Local Assemblies, to which savers were convened, created, especially in the first decade of CLP's existence, a strong popular feeling perfectly identified with the nature of the institution.*"

companies to be located on plots of land which have to be prepared are considered to be highly interesting.

• In our relations with other entities an attempt shall be made to stress concordant aspects and, particularly, with relation to Popularban the aim shall be to define what is possible in mutual activities, without our having to mortgage any important assets.

• The staff of Caja Laboral shall be progressively strengthened, by incorporating the capable management staff necessary.

e) As Caja Laboral Popular could only maintain, by direct financing, 20 to 25% of the bills transferred by the Group, it was necessary to negotiate, above all with Banco Popular in San Sebastian, significant lines of discount the value of which exceeded more than 50% of the resources available to Caja Laboral Popular. The loyalty of the Group to its own financial entity strengthened Caja Laboral Popular even at the cost of putting its financial viability at risk as it was created to operate through bank intermediation.

Durango Branch

f) The operations carried out by Caja Laboral Popular were established at standard market rates, both in borrowing and lending, in a strictly controlled scenario of financial activity, scarcely lacking in competition in the price of money and services. In this way the first feelings of being united were transmitted to the associated cooperatives, conceived under the same ideological suppositions, based on a promising financial entity which in its first decade began its generous contribution to the Country where its origins lay.

g) For more than 14 years the financial reserves of Lagun-Aro were deposited in full in CLP and for the first 8 years they represented more than 25% of all the deposits held.

h) Finally, for more than 20 years the Group guaranteed all Caja Laboral's operations, by the provision of 25% of share capital, which was established as an additional guarantee and appeared as such in all the balance sheets, adjusted from year to year.

At times it was difficult to understand how a credit institution could grow at such a rate whilst refusing to grant credit to its savers.

The stimulation necessarily came about through branch managers committed to the cooperative ideal. The drawing up from 1961 of the **Annual Business Plan** - which until 1967 was known as the Financial Plan - set the figures to be achieved and in this way every effort was made based on a target which it was a moral obligation to meet.

Advertising was characterised by the direct incentives offered, which at that time were a novel concept, with gifts given for maintaining a certain balance in a savings account or if the balance had risen by a certain amount over a month.

Later the compensations became more sophisticated and were cooperativised by the creation of the so-called **associated savings scheme**. This consisted basically in a type of savings account which paid a fixed rate of interest which rose from 2% in 1966 to 3.5% in 1975. At the end of the year a "return" oscillating between 1.25% and 2% was paid. As a whole, the total interest - at that time no tax was paid on capital income - went from 3.5% in 1966 to 5.5% in 1970; that year coincided with a policy of tough financial restrictions, the immediate consequence of which was to increase the incentive to make deposits, thus enabling further growth; 35.8% of growth was achieved, but in 1969 it had been 62.7% and in 1971 it also rose to 45.7%, in all types of credit balance.

The model of a return on savings with the Local Assemblies, to which savers were convened, created, especially in the first decade of CLP's existence, a strong popular feeling perfectly identified with the nature of the institution.

There was a clear awareness that the Caja was "laboral" insofar as it transmitted the message that labour was the only resource capable of extolling, developing and creating well- being; as far as its "popular" character was concerned, the Caja was born in the midst of a people to whose intelligence it appealed in order to administer its resources, inform them of its management and pay back, in the form of social benefits, cooperative employment and community wealth - rather than by direct interest payments - the confidence which its savers had placed in Caja Laboral Popular.

This was the decade destined to protect the cooperativisation of savings and its unity. The best qualified men were assigned to the task, decisions necessary to strengthen the Caja were adopted and an appeal was made to society to mediate with those communities capable of understanding its message of working in solidarity, open to the continually unsatisfied cravings of society.

Pamplona, the Regional Office for Navarra.

At the end of 1970 the most indicative figures for Caja Laboral Popular and the Associated Group were as follows:

- in millions of pesetas -

Sales of the Associated Group	**6,348**
Exports	**786**
Personnel	**8,743**
Profit	
(7,8% over sales, once fixed dividends had been deducted)	**258**
Credit Balance in CLP	**3,204**
Total Liabilities CLP	**4,432**
Capital + Reserves CLP	
(without accumulating profit for the year)	**278**
Capital Adequacy Ratio	
(without accumulating profit for the year)	**8.7%**
Net profits of CLP for the year	**95**

From 1966 to 1970, in just four years, the Group's profits were 1.91 times higher and those of CLP 12.1 times higher.

In the meantime, credit liabilities, a basic measurement to assess the importance of financial intermediation, were 4.85 times higher, whilst the sales of the Group, in comparison with credit liabilities, were 2.2 times higher.

Progressively the figures were objectively showing the protection afforded by the associated Group to the Caja, in the unceasing search for financial self-sufficiency; if in 1966 the total resources of CLP represented 26% of the turnover of the Group, in 1970 they accounted for 70%.

3.3 THE CONSOLIDATION PERIOD: FROM 1971 TO 1980

From 1971 Caja Laboral began to be a power in its own right and to have sufficient resources to finance easily all the needs of the Group, modifying the balance of forces which bound its close institutional and commercial relations.

Whilst Caja Laboral increased its volume of resources 16 fold in ten years, the sales of the Group were 9.8 times higher. These increases were continually favourable to Caja Laboral and were the reason behind its consolidation as a financial institution.

Credit cooperativism, well established in Europe through the Raiffeisen Savings Bank in Germany and the Popular and Rural Savings Banks in Italy, had not managed to create a sound image amongst Spanish financial institutions.

The excessive influence which Trade Union Organizations (Obra Sindical de Cooperación) had over them, especially over the provincial Savings Banks, left this field of credit unprotected and meant that it suffered greatly when it later went through a process of revitalisation.

One of the main reasons behind the chronic weakness of these entities was that they were not subject to solvent inspection. The fact that they were directly dependent on the Ministry of Work, which lacked the means to correct deviations, and the general lack of standards to discipline credit and to consolidate the structure of the balance sheets, meant that during this decade there was a disproportionate accumulation of credits and guarantees in favour of few customers, which, by definition, constituted an objective increase in risk.

In the early sixties an attempt was made to pass the task of inspection to the **Official Credit Institute**, but this body was not up to the task either as it lacked the mechanisms, standards and staff to carry out this work effectively.

It was with a law of June 1971 dealing with the organisation of official credit, that Credit Cooperativism began to form part of the financial sector, and, like Banks and Savings

Banks was to be supervised by the Bank of Spain. Inspections were made in Caja Laboral Popular in 1972 and 1979 and the resulting reports confirmed, as expected, that the management had been correct, although CLP was obliged to eliminate the **Collective Voluntary Contributions** scheme because the returns, in the inspectors' opinion, could only be applied to members' operations; and the savers, of course, were not members.

At the same time in the sphere of financial discipline, investment, cash and capital adequacy ratios were established in support of the Government's sectorial financing policy, of liquidity and solvency, respectively. But by the end of the decade there were certain institutional support mechanisms in favour of Credit Cooperatives, basically with respect to

Inside the Head Offices.

making them more profitable - a lower non remunerated cash ratio - doubtlessly because the sector, in addition to having been conceived with a certain degree of paternalism was not profitable or sound either, due to this feeble protection.

Caja Laboral Popular began to make itself felt due to the amount of savings it attracted for its financing operations.

At the start of the decade, in 1970, 54% of deposits in the Basque Country were in Banks, 44% in Savings Banks and barely 2% in CLP; but by the end of 1980 CLP had managed to attract 5.6%.

The number of branches grew from 52 in 1970 to 102 in 1980. This demonstrated, within the regional scope of its social statutes, an agile consolidation in tune, firstly, with the expansion of the associated cooperatives further afield and then, with a continuous process of opening new branches, propitiated by the excellent reception it got and by the desire to reach a minimum capacity which, reducing costs, would project CLP in a framework of sustained and autonomous profitability.

As Caja Laboral increased its protagonism, in direct relation to its financial and economic capacity, it began to occupy a position of greater ascendency over the Group.

In May 1970 a document was studied entitled **"conditions required"** (for) **Association with Caja Laboral Popular** of the cooperatives so desiring. A model of reference was required to dispel the discretionary nature of the decisions of the Governing Council when it came to judging whether or not to accept new cooperatives, the only entities, together with their members, with the legal right to join CLP.

However the very close links between the Financial Institution and its Associated Group and the reciprocal exclusiveness with respect to financing, required a document which would establish legal, technical and doctrinal concepts which the cooperatives would be obliged to respect: the practical manifestation of these principles in capital remuneration, members' contributions and the distribution of profit; those dealing with work structure; the significance of the cooperatives' commitment to the rest of the labour world and society in general. It was also necessary to establish an adequate means of periodically channelling information about the commercial development of the cooperatives which, moreover, CLP had to be able to control through their own audits.

In various meetings held on 4th, 5th, 22nd and 23rd December 1975, this project was formulated by representatives of the cooperatives. It was subjected to significant modifications because, in the last analysis, the idea was to establish, imperatively, a common practice. And although official confirmation was given to what had been unofficial practice until then, what was achieved by means of a voluntarily made agreement did not have the same coercive force as simple honest intentions, subject to the hazards of dialectical situations created by circumstance. This was how the so-called **Contract of Association** was born. It was approved at the Extraordinary General Assembly held on 10th July 1976 and has lasted in the same terms until 1990.

The consolidation of CLP came at the right time. In 1973 the price of oil based fuel increased four fold and in 1979 doubled again. We were on the verge of significant events which were to upset the world economy and more so the Spanish economy, due to its greater fragility.

"*From 1971 Caja Laboral began to be a power in its own right and to have sufficient resources to finance easily all the needs of the Group, modifying the balance of forces which bound its close institutional and commercial relations.*"

Lan Kide 3 building.

But at the close of 1980, the objective figures demonstrating CLP's relationship with its almost exclusive clientele, were as follows:

	- in millions of pesetas -
Sales of the Associated Group	69,064
Exports	13,576
Personnel	18,733
Profit	
(9% over sales, once fixed dividends had been deducted)-	415
Credit Balance in CLP	51,425
Total Liabilities CLP	66,758
Capital + Reserves CLP	
(without accumulating profit for the year)	5,016
Capital Adequacy Ratio	
(without accumulating profit for the year)	9.75%
Net profits of CLP for the year	1,314

As can be appreciated, CLP's total resources were almost equivalent to the sales of the Group, and profits, at the start of an unprecedented phase of recession, were extraordinarily positive, although for the Group they were negative for the first time.

In early February 1974 CLP's headquarters were transferred to a plot of land on a hillside known as Olandixo, in Mondragón.

This was the culmination of a phase of development which later included the Data Processing Centre, Ikerlan, Lagun-Aro, the Business Division (LKS) and the Olandixo "farmhouse" which serves as a dining and lodgings facility for visitors.

Changing tack, the regional vocation of Caja Laboral Popular was clearly secured now that it was located close to the slopes of Besaide, a mountain which is the meeting point of the provinces of Vizcaya, Alava and Guipuzcoa. But as the eighties approached, a process of administrative decentralisation began with regional headquarters established in Bilbao (Arenal), Vitoria (Dato), San Sebastian and Pamplona, turning on its head the organisation which until then had been centralised in Mondragón.

From a normative point of view and in a vicissitudinary fashion, CLP progressively gained the express recognition of Government. Until then Government had not accepted the guarantee of Credit Cooperatives, with a view to supporting credits of the Banco de Credito Industrial. It also placed obstacles in the way of relations with the Treasury and in acting as collectors for the Social Security system, and the same was true for other organs of State. Government was obstinately set on excluding them from any legal framework by expressly stating that the only bodies qualified were Banks and Savings Banks although these, in objective terms, offered less guarantees than those offered by CLP.

At the same time the Bank of Spain conceded CLP lines of rediscount which meant that CLP's dependence and the Bank of Spain's support were regularised. CLP's margin of liquidity improved and its profitability was strengthened still more. But, above all, Caja Laboral Popular had come of age as a financial institution.

3.4 THE CHALLENGES OF TIME: 1981 TO 1990

The decade had two different yet complementary parts: On the one hand the first half of the decade was characterised by a strong commitment on the part of CLP to the economic and financial development of the Group in a situation ravaged by the economy as a result of the two oil crises.

The immediate effects were a reduction in the growth of GDP to below 1%, when it had been 6% in the previous period; a resurgence of inflation at an average rate of increase of 16.6% between 1974 and 1983. But the most poignant and disturbing consequences, as far as the social balance in the Basque Country was concerned, came about as a result of the devastating unemployment figures of 25%, which condemned to inactivity more than 250,000 capable men and women, who were only too eager to work.

Support mechanisms to overcome this situation were set in motion by various actions taken by the Group: the cooperatives reduced and even halted increases in wages and also required further capital contributions from members; Lagun-Aro created its "employment aid" benefit; and Caja Laboral Popular deployed mechanisms of solidarity, reducing the cost of money and continuing to create new cooperatives and taking steps with those already associated to mitigate unemployment and even increase workforces, taking a direction completely contrary to what was occurring on the rest of the industrial stage.

Measures were taken to establish a policy of support for the Associated Group. The first, taken early in 1980, reduced the interest on loans to have a favourable effect on the financial costs of the cooperatives whose borrowing was increasing over advisable levels. These measures can only be explained in terms of the positive feeling of solidarity amassed over the twenty previous years, during which CLP was obliged to turn to the Group. This measure was followed by another based on tougher criteria in tune with the vicissitudes of the Group which in 1984, hitting rock bottom, saw its turnover fall by 3%. The measure taken by CLP consisted of offering the cooperatives interest-free loans to a value equivalent to 4% of total liabilities.

Finally, always based on the restrictive maxim, implying reciprocal responsibility, **Caja = Cooperative = Members**, a financing scheme was devised capable of returning the balance sheets to normality by restructuring the cooperatives affected. The protection mechanisms meant that CLP completely absorbed the insolvency of some cooperatives, whilst the members of these cooperatives agreed to reduce their wages to about 80%, or even 70% of what they would normally have earned. But above all companies were restructured with staffing adjustments, renewal of production equipment and changes in management.

During these episodes the information received through the Contract of Association, the Business Division and Lagun-Aro's recently established "employment aid" benefit played a basic role.

The volume of aid given by Caja Laboral through the reduction in interest rates and the cancellation of debts totalled 16,000 million pesetas, over nearly 10 years, in the form of transfers from its funds to those of the Group. But in spite of all this, CLP maintained its net profitability over total liabilities above 2%, almost double that obtained by banks in the same period. And, what is more revealing, the Associated Group grew from 18,733 jobs in 1980 to 20,409 in 1987, when in the same period more than 150,000 jobs were lost in the Basque Country.

The Contract of Association, the devastating effects of an economy in crisis, the financial and economic efforts of Caja Laboral Popular to return its equity to a situation of equilibrium, the prudent actions of management, more alert to what might happen in the future economically speaking, the conviction that joining forces offered a stronger position and the banking sector was engaged in a search for new critical dimensions, all advised, from 1982, that a new order be established in Caja Laboral Popular's relations with the Group, and in the Group's internal relations.

The second part of the decade saw the Group's return to profitability. This reduced the pressure on Caja Laboral in its tenacious effort to create a Special Insolvency Fund to compensate the excess risk latent in the Group. In the Long Term Plan for the period 1986 to 1990, 0.9% over average assets was earmarked for provisions, calculated for the five year period at 12,124 million pesetas, as an enormous precautionary measure. But it proved unnecessary.

The world economy recovered, the price of energy returned, in relative terms, to previous levels and in Spain a political regime was established which promoted a clear improvement in the economy with 5% increases in GDP. Companies began to breathe more easily and net profits began to flow. The most immediate result was seen in the financial independence ratio of the aggregate balance sheet for the Group which jumped from 0.47 in 1984 to 0.70 in 1988, a clear reflection of a lesser level of indebtedness in relation to equity.

However the deep recession which occurred in the second half of the decade of the seventies had had a profound effect on financial intermediaries. Deposit Guarantee Funds were created for Banks and Savings Banks. The Fund for Banks had to act decisively to close or merge some institutions and reestablish equilibrium in a large number of others.

The Credit Cooperative Fund was created somewhat later. Caja Laboral Popular asked for it to be set up on 18th November 1981, but it was not established until October of the following year.

Twenty-odd credit cooperatives were revitalised by means of a Plan of 5th March 1984 drawn up by a Government Commission for Economic Affairs, which consisted of interest free credits to be returned over a period of five years. But a large number of cooperatives disappeared, especially rural ones, due to the somewhat reckless fashion in which some of these cooperatives were artificially created. At this time Caja Laboral Popular accounted for more than 20% of the volume of deposits of the one hundred or so Credit Cooperatives in Spain. There was firm proof of its solvency, creating a positive deferential climate because its investment policy had kept faith with the basic concept of providing finance for cooperative companies and because its strict capitalization of profits provided protection in the light of an excellent balance sheet situation.

Inside the Lan Kide 3 building.

In 1986 Spain joined the European Economic Community adding more elements to the debate going on in the Group as a result of the strained situation prevalent during the long period of recession. Later on 1st July 1987 came the start of the process towards the Single European Market, to create a Europe without economic frontiers.

At the same time the financial weight of Caja Laboral had been completely dedicated to the Group. However, as we have seen, its financial capacity, insufficient at the start, clearly began to be more than sufficient in the period 1980- 1990. In 1964 investments in the Group accounted for 67% of all its resources; in 1970 this figure was nearer 50%; in 1980 it was 36%; it scarcely totalled 23% in 1985, and at the end of 1990 it only amounted to 10.5%. It should be borne in mind that specific bank investment accounted for 50% of resources on the balance sheet, the other half destined towards maintaining high levels under the cash and bank balances heading, when transfers for compulsory investments were made and to the operational fixed assets heading.

For this reason in Caja Laboral Popular, to ensure that its investment programmes continued to comply with its own basic concepts and current legislation, investment programmes in housing cooperatives (started back in 1973) and educational cooperatives were activated.

There were 20 such housing cooperatives which resulted in the construction of more than 1,200 homes. As far as the ikastolas (Basque schools) were concerned, whilst they remained part of the private sector until midway through the decade, 46 of them were associated, with a total of 46,000 students.

The time had come to open the doors to individual credit. Caja Laboral's philosophy of giving priority to community over individual credit - *"the promotion of man through the community"* - because of insufficient means and the tortuous problem of having to make all savers members to be able to grant them loans, had to be adapted to the new social and economic situation.

On 20th April 1982 a request was made to the Ministry of Work to enable 15% of total resources to be applied to third parties. Authorization was given at the end of November that year. This 15% accounted for 40% of bank investment. Thus CLP began to break with its policy of purely cooperative investment, because, above all, the economic recession had drawn attention to the dangers of concentrating credit and because, in any case, the surplus resources held by CLP had to be distributed to compensate for the potential investment bias towards the Group.

This opening up turned out to be greater with the encouragement of the Bank of Spain and the Ministry of Economy and Finance. In April 1987 the latest General Law on Cooperatives came into being, ever more open to breaking with one of the classic rules of cooperativism: the mutual nature of operations in relation to the members.

However, one of the law's provisions made the following stipulation *"Until the new regulations are established ..."*, but a significant opening had been created enabling 15% of total resources to be dedicated to non-members and solutions were contrived whereby the profits from these operations were assigned to compulsory non-distributable reserves.

This constituted the basis for the enactment of **Law 13/1989 on Credit Cooperatives** on 26th May 1989. This law overcame limitations to the expansion of credit cooperatives, breaking with two specific limitations.

a) The first broke the so-called "adjectival" mould whereby to be a **beneficiary of credit**, membership was essential and to be a member, associated companies had to be cooperatives, and individuals, members of associated cooperatives. With this new Law, credit cooperatives began to have their own vitality, in that they could be credit cooperatives although they had not been created by other cooperatives, and were able to carry out operations with third parties who were not members, even if it were at the expense of tax benefits.

b) The second, which stopped **sovereignty** being bound to the services provided or to the number of members the associates had, stated as follows: "members' votes may be proportional to their contribution to nominal capital"...

The aim of both of these measures was to remedy a situation considered adverse.

As for financing third parties, this widened the field of credit, spread risk and objectively reduced the danger of mistakes in the Caja's operations.

With regard to the right to exercise the power to administer the cooperative in terms of the contribution made to its capitalization, this corrected the problem of potential restraints on members due to a lack of sufficient capital or when trying to remedy critical situations with respect to their economic performance.

In the second half of the five year period, at the end of 1990, CLP found itself in the following situation:

a) The Group could be financed with less than 10% of Caja Laboral's resources and, moreover, the growth in its credit capacity was growing at a greater rate than the objective needs of the cooperatives.

b) Caja Laboral Popular's size, with 400,000 million pesetas of total resources, was equivalent to 140% of Group sales and its profits were similar to those obtained by the Group, excluding Lagun-Aro.

c) Caja Laboral Popular's preeminent role, maintained by the positive and dissuasive force of its financial capacity, had been transferred to the Group, which had created its own organs: the **General Council** and the **Congress of the Mondragon Cooperative Group** at the end of 1984. This situation was what the Group wanted, assigning Caja Laboral Popular the role of cooperative specialising in credit within the spectrum of cooperative options.

d) Caja Laboral is faced with a clearly promising future, although tinged with inevitable uncertainty. To its sufficient size and vigorous development, in growth and in the profitability which reinforces it, must be added the responsibility of being part of a scenario which is more supervised, more competitive and, as a result, more technical than ever.

e) However Caja Laboral Popular has stood out for its social vocation which *"...has to pay constant and serious attention to whatever may arise in the social sectors of existing organisations: cooperativism must be considered as a vanguard element of the workers' movement and all workers should be able to benefit from the results of cooperative training and administrative experience, to improve, study and project their problems".*

In 1987 there was a change in the General Management, which had been appointed early in 1961 and, in February 1989, in the Chairmanship, which had been appointed soon after. This biological change formed part of a vital transformation and moreover, although it may not seem so, through thorough daily examination, expectations and ambitions change.

As Caja Laboral Popular has grown at a greater rate than the Group it finances, it has developed ever less cooperative investment, whilst mutual dependence has slackened, with activities involving small and medium sized companies, domestic economies and even public institutions beginning to take on more importance.

The provisions of the Law of May 1989 have extended - contrary to strictly cooperative principles - the options for exercising sovereignty in management bodies. The banking deregulation carried out by the Ministry of Economy and the Bank of Spain has given CLP, like other institutions, the universal capacity to operate as a financial intermediary. Moreover, access to the European Community - planned for 1st January 1993 - adds new factors of potential competition to be taken into account.

The significance of all this is that Caja Laboral Popular is faced with a magnificent stage on which to continue working based on its tradition and on which to project the mission it was originally assigned. The options of this mission are still valid because they belong to the sphere of moral and solidary behaviour on which CLP has successfully based its 31 years of existence.

At the end of 1990 CLP's figures were as follows:

	- in millions of pesetas -
Sales of the Associated Group	**(*) 299,231**
Exports	**(*) 54,808**
Personnel	**(*) 22,860**
Profit	
(3.54% over sales, once fixed dividends had been deducted)	**(*) 10,631**
Credit Balance in CLP	**311,112**
Total Liabilities CLP	**397,452**
Capital + Reserves CLP	
(without accumulating profit for the year)	**28,384**
Capital Adequacy Ratio	
(without accumulating profit for the year)	**9.81%**
Net profits of CLP for the year	**5,575**

(*) **Forecasts**

EXECUTIVE STRUCTURE OF CAJA LABORAL POPULAR UP TO 1987

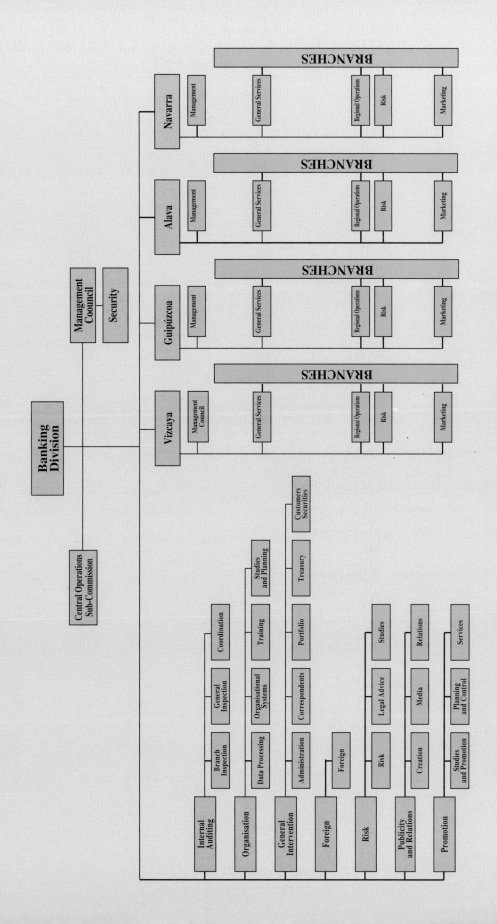

EXECUTIVE STRUCTURE OF CAJA LABORAL POPULAR
(From 1987)

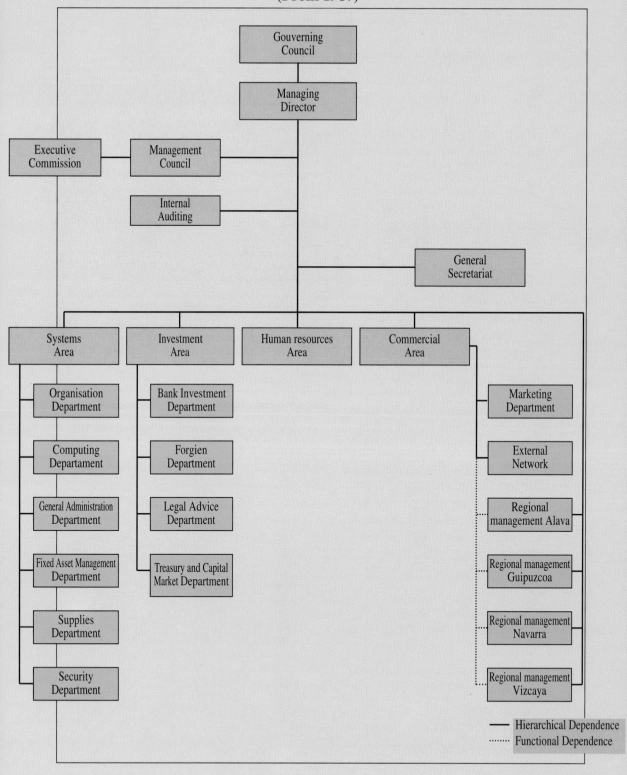

3.5 THE BUSINESS DIVISION

This division started life, when CLP was born, as a *"technical service"* (article 2 of the Statutes), on the same modest level which characterises all the initiatives undertaken in the early days of the experience.

From 1962 it found a place in the Business Plan, in which notice was given of the cohesive character pursued by Caja Laboral Popular, working from this department on the Associated Group.

In the period ending in 1969 the work of this department consisted practically in the support which it was able to give the Management Committee of Ulgor, whose members doubled up by occupying posts in both this cooperative and Caja Laboral.

Technical Office with the Amboto peak in the background.

At that time the activities were almost of a management nature, giving support to the creation and consolidation of cooperatives from within.

In this way the following cooperatives were born: **Copreci, Ederlan, Arrasate, Lana, Soraluce and Eroski** (originally Comerco). Some were the result of internal initiatives and others of external ones: **URSSA, Vicon, Guria, Ulma, Matrici,** etc. were created in a climate of entrepreneurial emancipation and encouraged by the success of the Mondragon cooperatives, whose effects were beginning to be felt in nearby areas. All these companies were supported from the Business Division of CLP.

In January 1968, after eight years of experience, a key document was drawn up, which was definitively going to establish the identity of this "section", at the same time that its management took on a vitality of its own; nothing had yet been said about its institutional separation from Caja Laboral Popular, although the following was indeed set down:

"The Business Section should be autonomous and be set up in the direction of a second degree cooperative and, of course, not be called Business Section but have the name determined by the cooperatives which make up the industrial Complex which shall be integrated or federated".

These expectations were a premonition of what twenty years later was to be done with the Mondragon Cooperative Group.

That same document amply established the functions to be carried out. It is interesting to note that the departments created then covered the following functions:

1. Industrial Relations Area

- Legal matters, External relations, Production techniques, Research and patent rights.

2.Construction and Urban Development Area

- Sites, Urban development, Architecture.

3. Production Plant Study Area.

- Planning, Methods, Design.

4. Sectorial Promotion Area.

- Fishing, Agriculture, Consumer, Services

5. Labour Relations Area.

- Job organisation and assessment, Safety and Hygiene, Psychotechnics and Personnel selection, Training.

6. Studies Area.

- Analysis of economic situation and control, Legal Advice, Marketing Studies, Administration methods.

Starting from these definitions, the Division was developed under the current model which lasted twenty years until 1989.

At the end of 1970 and the start of 1971, on the basis of the way Caja Laboral Popular worked, it was defined as *"restricted"* only to cooperatives, *"different"* because it established more committed relations than those normally established in the sector, and *"limited"* - because if it expanded it would have to do so with other cooperatives and their members - as an entity which should project its Business Division exercising the following functions:

Precautionary:

Through the Group's Auditing and Economic Control Department to gain a thorough knowledge of the Group's performance.

Intervention:

By way of emergency support in favour of the cooperatives, although at that time the economic situation was strong, and

Promotion:

To draw up projects through a responsible group of promoters ... in order to carry out the industrial development intended under the cooperative formula.

In 1983 there was another restructuring. The new organisational structure detailed the following functions:

*The **Studies Area** of the Business Division has been created to carry out economic studies dealing with the situation within the cooperatives, the Basque Country, Spain and internationally and which shall serve, both for Caja Laboral Popular and for the Cooperative Group and various Institutions and people in the Basque Country, to aid decision making as regards development policy and integration in the multinational economy.*

*The **Agrofood Promotion Area** has been created to contribute to the development of this Cooperative Sector associated with Caja Laboral Popular, by means of studying the commercial viability of new cooperative enterprises and the development projects of existing ones and the technical-entrepreneurial advice necessary for the materialisation and consolidation of these new activities, and for the recovery of companies in crisis situations.*

*The **Industrial Promotion Area** has been created to search out and find new industrial products and activities capable of being taken on by new and existing cooperatives, as well as to provide advice to these enterprises in finding the right industrial development policies. In addition it shall advise new cooperatives promoted by Caja Laboral Popular in the creation and launch phases of their industrial activities.*

*The **Intervention Area** has been created to advise the associated cooperatives in their planning functions and in the management of such functions, as well as to intervene and/or provide assistance in actions designed to recover cooperatives in situations of crisis.*

*The **Consulting Area** has been created as a specialised services and functional assistance area for associated cooperatives to adapt the quality and organisation of their resources to the international demands of development and competition. Likewise, it shall collaborate with the Intervention, Industrial Promotion and Agrofood Promotion Areas in promotion activities and activities designed to assist cooperatives in crisis. It shall also contribute to the development of intercooperative structures and ties in the functional spheres and dimensions of enterprises.*

*The **Auditing and Information Area** has been created to monitor the business situation and management results of, and development prospects for, cooperatives at an individual level and groups by gathering, analyzing and assessing all the information available. Likewise, it has been created to analyze and evaluate Caja Laboral Popular's risk in the associated cooperatives and to study the investment operations which these cooperatives ask of Caja Laboral Popular, comparing and verifying the net worth of the cooperatives with the accounting information provided to Caja Laboral Popular in compliance with the Contract of Association.*

*The **Urban Development and Construction Area** has been created to provide the associated cooperatives (industrial, agricultural, housing, etc.) with the urban infrastructure and the* *buildings and installations required to carry out their specific activities and aims. Likewise, it shall offer its Civil Engineering services to associated cooperatives in technology transfer and joint venture operations. As a complementary activity, it shall also attend to companies, institutions and centres of a social character or of interest to the Cooperative Group.*

At the start of the seventies the figure of 0.25% of Caja Laboral Popular's average total liabilities was set as the maximum limit which this entity would annually assign to promote cooperative development through the Business Division. This limit was a relatively important figure equivalent to 15% of some excellent results.

From 1972 the cooperatives were directly charged for certain services, and these charges covered approximately 65% of the cost, accounting for 0.23% of CLP's budget in 1978 and dropping to 0.069% in 1988.

1986 saw the start of a process of reflection on the future of the Business Division, whose structure and operation was at that time based on the following:

a) One of the characteristics which has best defined Caja Laboral Popular and reflected its vocation for creating employment, is its *Business Division*. This institution is unlikely to be found in the heart of any other financial intermediary, but it is necessary and can be explained by the specific nature of its original vocation and is included in the regulations covering credit cooperatives.

b) The sluggish period of investment experienced by the Group after the deep recession suffered from 1975 to 1985 meant that the Business Division directed its market, first towards public institutions - Town Halls, Provincial Councils, the Basque Government - and, later, towards private customers.

c) During the periods in which intervention was necessary in the cooperatives, in the aforementioned decade of recession, it was demonstrated that the activities of the Business Division, as a technical instrument, inevitably committed Caja Laboral Popular as a financial instrument.

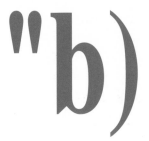

Caja Laboral Popular's size, with 400,000 million pesetas of total resources, was equivalent to 140% of Group sales and its profits were similar to those obtained by the Group, excluding Lagun-Aro."

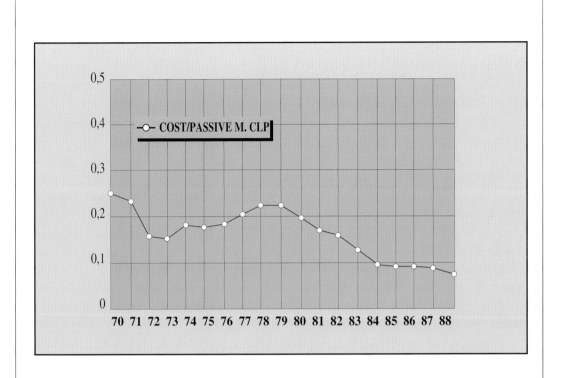

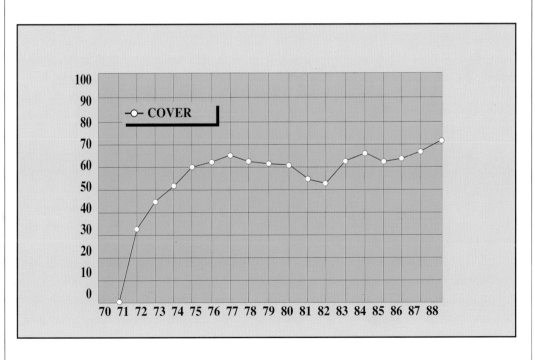

Adverse situations occurred in which Caja Laboral Popular took responsibility due to its economic strength, whilst the associated cooperatives, in a climate of anxiety and general deterioration of the industrial and social fabric, strove to pass on the cost of their economic rehabilitation to Caja Laboral Popular.

d) In 1987 there was a change in the General Management of Caja Laboral Popular, and the Business Division was installed in a new building on the Olandixo hillside. It was becoming ever clearer that it was necessary for the Business Division to have its own legal status - to be able to operate in an open market.

So initially a company, *LKS, S.A.*, was created as a stepping stone, and was still operating in 1990, especially in dealings with third parties.

e) In general the Business Division enjoys a level of prestige, through the Report on the Basque Economy which was edited by the Studies Area from 1976 to 1988, and because the Group survived the crisis period without, in spite of everything, significant social and economic upsets. However, there also arose, after the tensions involved in carrying out the restructuring of various cooperatives and groups, a certain degree of human dissatisfaction which attracted criticism of its conduct and the way it operated.

In this situation, first its separation from CLP was tackled, a subject which had been foreseen in 1968, and then its elimination.

The process followed was, in short, as follows:

1) *The Industrial Construction and Urban Development, and Consulting Areas*, with more than 55 members, combined to form an associated worker cooperative which under the name LKS, S. Coop. would offer engineering services: civil, urban development, construction, housing, turn-key plants and property valuations; consulting services: strategic advice, marketing, legal advice, tax, financial, human resources and production engineering. The prospects are that this cooperative, to be integrated in the Group, will be profitable, with complete autonomy in its activities and management.

2) *The Auditing part of the Auditing and Information Area* was formed into a separate company in 1988, specifically devoted to offering auditing services, so that its functions complied with the Spanish Law on Account Auditing of 12th July 1988.

3) *The Industrial and Agricultural Promotion, the Information and the Intervention Areas* were kept on as part of the Central Services of the General Council, the executive body of the Mondragon Cooperative Group.

4) *The Studies Area* was included in the direct services of Caja Laboral Popular (previously the Banking Division).

By the end of 1990 the Business Division had disappeared and its members had dispersed to join one of four different work centres, with the most recognisable expression of its past being the *Consultoria LKS*.

GENERAL ORGANISATIONAL CHART OF THE BUSINESS DIVISION (1980)

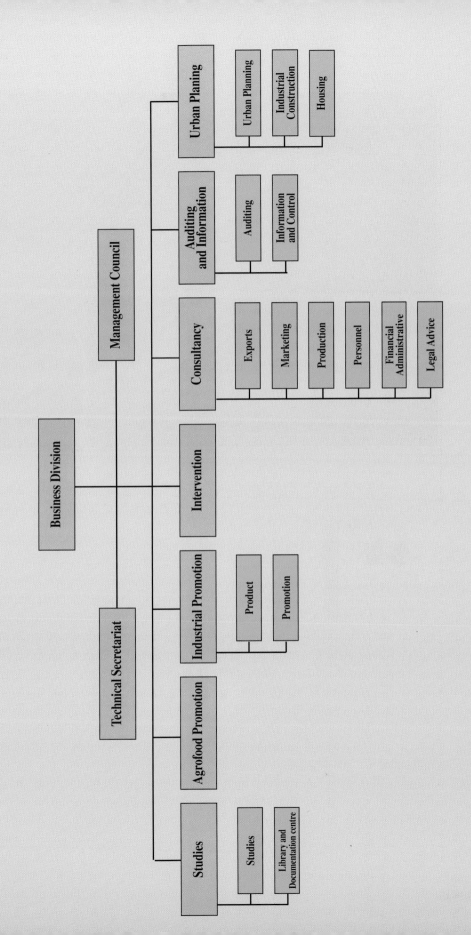

"Today individuals mean so little, that to keep their personality they have to submerge themselves and even to a certain extent disappear in associations, because, just as the drop of water which wants to keep its personality has to disappear into the ocean, because otherwise it would evaporate in the atmosphere, individuals need the help and support of others. (J.Mª Arizmendiarrieta)"

4. LAGUN-ARO: VOLUNTARY SOCIAL WELFARE ENTITY

4.1 THE COOPERATIVE RESPONSE TO A LACK OF COVER

From 1955 all that was developed in the sphere of social welfare for cooperative members complied with the Law covering Social Security, according to which ... *"individuals and family members dependent on them, are guaranteed adequate protection, in contingencies and situations and are guaranteed the progressive raising of their standard of living in health, economic and cultural terms".*

However, on 15th December 1958, in a ruling of the Ministry of Work, cooperative members were excluded from the General Social Security System in Spain.

This Government decision was the key element to the start of a period of reflection which progressively led to a search for a system of cover for cooperative members, a system which is today **Lagun-Aro.**

The fact that the average age of the census was quite young at 30, meant that bold projections could be made as long term or life annuity benefits would not be potentially claimed for thirty five years.

There were other factors besides this crude and immature forecast.

The three cooperatives which undertook this task were: Ulgor, Arrasate, and Funcor. By the end of 1959 they had 320 members between them. They professed great confidence in the founding directors, and the economic results, which were excellent, created a set of expectations which were circumstantially favourable.

Regulations were completed forthwith in the head offices of Funcor and Ulgor to provide the *Social Welfare Service* on 1st October 1959.

At the same time Caja Laboral Popular had applied to the Ministry of Work to be registered as a Credit Cooperative *" to provide financial, technical and social services for Talleres Arrasate, Talleres Ulgor and the San José Cooperative of Mondragón, Funcor of Elorrio and any other technical, producer or craft cooperatives which may subsequently become members".*

As "social services" was one of CLP's aims, the **Social Welfare Service** was created. On 16th July 1959 Caja Laboral Popular's registration with the Ministry of Work was approved providing the legal cover for the birth of Lagun-Aro. This all occurred even before, as we shall see, Caja Laboral began to offer its "financial services" to the associated cooperatives, which was the main reason for which the Credit Cooperative had been formed.

4.2 COOPERATIVE BASED SELF-INSURANCE MODELS

1959-1967: Individual and Insufficient Cover

Given the strength of spirit behind the still incipient development of the industrial cooperatives, it was possible to demand committed models for social cover.

*"The structure of the Social Welfare Service is based on maximum **responsibility** and **personal autonomy** in support of the **human and christian solidarity** of each of the working communities"*. Thus read, somewhat indicatively and pedagogically, article 3 of the Regulations, the "magna carta" for the social cover created.

At this time Lagun-Aro was one of the services of Caja Laboral Popular. It was autonomously controlled through its Management Commission but strictly responsible to the Governing Council and General Assembly of Caja Laboral Popular.

The financial cover for the benefits was very weak. In view of the profits obtained by the cooperatives which were allocated to the individual contributions of the members, it was thought that these would be the basis of the life annuity benefits, when members reached retirement age.

Not to enter into a complex explanation and by way of a summary, it can be said that the model had two systems of finance which in turn corresponded to the nature of the benefit.

a) Compensable benefits, so-called because they were paid in situations giving a right to temporary aid, included sickness benefit - which covered sick leave and sickness expenses -, marriage allowance, death benefit, birth benefit and family allowance.

25% of the wages of each member were transferred to a personal account - hence their being called personal contributions -, and when members had compensable expenses to pay they used the balance in these accounts by means of refunds controlled by the Service.

Only 70% of sick leave expenses and between 80 and 95% of sickness and prescription costs were refunded.

At the end of the year, a balance was made of the economic situation of each member and for the Service as a whole. 35% of the personal income created with the 25% paid by each member was deducted from each and every member. This money was used to create **the solidarity fund** which served to make up the balances of those members who had spent in excess with regard to benefits. This compensation was carried out on the basis of calculating, for the year, the average expenses of the members. The solidarity quota paid by the members enabled up to 85% of the difference to be made up between each member's refunded expenses and the average expenses, in the same year, of all the members.

These benefits, which in all friendly societies are financed by the **pro rata system**, were a strict source of deficit for members on lower incomes, with large families prone to ill-health.

They had in their favour the fact that they encouraged individual effort on the part of those lucky enough not to incur expenses. However they were not completely solidary, despite forming part of a period marked by an impulsive cooperativism in which an attempt was made to establish, on a permanent basis, responsibility on the part of

Inside the Head Offices

members and workers for the development and situation of their company.

b) The **so-called rebatable benefits** were those which, being life annuity benefits, were financed by the system of individualised capitalization. Each member paid 5% of his wages to a fund "destined for Old Age Benefit".

The main intention was to cover old age or retirement, leaving widowhood and orphanage uncovered, in relative terms.

Members had necessarily to reach the age of 65 or be "declared disabled" after the age of 45 to qualify.

The sum of the deposits made with the 5% contribution plus the annual interest and the excess which members may have had in their individual compensable benefit account formed the basis for how the retirement pension was financed.

This pension was calculated by means of a rate table which was established, in economic terms, in the following way:

- For every 100 pesetas contributed at the age of 14 (which would have been deposited over 51 years at a 4% rate of interest) an annual pension of 125.12 pesetas was guaranteed.

- For every 100 pesetas contributed at the age of 65 (zero deposit time) the annual pension was 11.09 pesetas.

- Between both extremes the pensions resulting for the remaining years were in proportion to the time transpired from the date on which the deposit was made. The sum of all the pension fractions gave the total pension.

This system was the passionate and doubtlessly unconscious fruit of a period of cooperative euphoria far from the implacable reality of the randomness of situations leading to the right to pensions, especially those of widowhood and orphanage, which, although they were covered, always ended up with the widows having to join the cooperative, taking over their husbands' jobs.

It was soon clear that the system, known in vulgar terms, as the "account" system, did not provide sufficient protection.

The performance of the cooperatives entered a period of relative decline and their capacity to form the financial basis for retirement widowhood and orphanage benefits, plus disability benefits, did not appear to be the same. The complement to these pensions, which, it had been hoped, would be high due to returns paid on the magnificent results of the cooperatives, dropped considerably and ceased to be a solid and solvent factor, becoming instead a purely random addendum.

1967-today: Social Security as a Complement to Lagun-Aro

Eight years of experience led to the following basic conclusions:

a) Pensions should be guaranteed irrespective of the economic and financial performance of each member's cooperative.

b) Life annuity benefits should not be of a random amount: All members should know in advance what pension they are going to receive on retirement according to their contracts. The same for cases of disability, widowhood and orphanage.

c) Such pensions, although taking into account the amount in the capital accounts held by members in their cooperatives, should be similar to those that employed workers received through the Spanish Social Security System.

The current system used by Lagun-Aro was first proposed in 1967, although still as part of Caja Laboral Popular through its Social Welfare Service.

The new Lagun-Aro Social Security system came into being on 21st January 1968, in a General Assembly which lasted more than 10 hours due to the high number of interventions to clarify points and of proposals for alternative wording.

A large scale effort had been made in communication, information and consultation to establish the details of the system which was going to affect, especially in the long term, the social economies of the cooperators or the family members who survived them.

Solidarity was more evident and the system began, although somewhat late, to be more technical and appropriate; although the responsibility of the worker/member was not lost from sight.

The new system was based on three levels of solidarity:

a) All the annual contributions shall be the same for all members depending on their respective income, the same as with the level of benefit, and both contributions and benefits shall be decided, annually, in the General Assembly. *First level of solidarity*: All members have the same options.

b) Each working community - initially each cooperative and then groups of cooperatives - shall be able to take advantage of the benefits agreed in the General Assembly. If the members in a community surpass 110% of the average benefits calculated per year, the difference shall be made up by the members affected, and if the figure is below 100%, Lagun-Aro shall return 50% of the difference. *Second level of solidarity:* The members of each working community shall demonstrate solidarity with each other.

c) All members shall pay a fraction of their expenses with respect to sickness benefit and sick leave. *Third level of solidarity:* All members are responsible, to a certain extent, for their own expenses.

Based on this criteria two different types of benefits were established and are still in force today. The difference between them lies in the way they are financed.

1) Pro rata

The so-called **pro rata** benefits specify the irrevocable right to these benefits which are settled up for all members from year to year. Expenses incurred by all members are distributed proportionately, and if at the end of the year more has been spent on benefits than contributions paid, contributions are raised so that they are made up for the following year.

The opposite occurs if expenses are less than contributions paid.

This financing model covers:

- Health care

- Sick leave

- Family allowance

In 1990 the contributions were as follows:

- Health care: 6,610 pesetas/month

- Sick leave: 3.85% of wages

- Family allowance: 1,470 pesetas/month

2) Collective Capitalization

The so-called **collective capitalization** benefits have turned out to be more complicated in their establishment and in their application. Factors which are difficult to reduce to precise terms come into play in their calculation because these benefits are based on initial suppositions which have to be modified with time, but whose rate of variation is impossible to know.

At the time this model was being studied, there was a change in legislation dealing with social welfare for cooperative members.

On 30th May 1962 the Statutes of the Mutualidad de Autonomos (State Agency providing Social Security cover for the self-employed) were approved and in Rulings dated 25th m March and 7th October 1963, the Ministry of Work made it compulsory for members of all cooperatives to affiliate to this agency.

With the backing of our already created Welfare Service, the Group Associated with Caja Laboral Popular resisted affiliation, asking above all for a Special System to be established, different from that for the self-employed, for all cooperators who were members of associated worker cooperatives (at that time members of industrial cooperatives).

However it was not just the imperative of the Law which forced definitive affiliation to the Mutualidad de Autonomos: twelve years had gone by since the creation of the first industrial cooperative and 1967 turned out to be a year of forewarning.

Added to the fact that cooperators had to guarantee their life annuity pensions through collective capitalization, calculated by means of a suitable actuarial study, it must also be pointed out that there were potential risks which members could incur if a private body like the Welfare Service should fail in its calculations, either due to a general drop in the number of members, or because of incorrect budgeting or, faced with an always uncertain future, owing to the long period before some benefits came into force. There was no reason for the managers at that time to take on, in a way difficult to rationalise, the responsibility for having to affiliate later, due to unforeseeable circumstances, to a Social Security System whose benefits were and are guaranteed and administered by the State.

The meetings held and the differences of opinion maintained between 1963 and 1967 with the Ministry of Work are an example of the desire to maintain total independence for the Welfare Service from the State Social Security System. But in 1967 an agreement was finally reached with the Director General for Welfare on 14th September *"authorising the Mutualidad Laboral de Trabajadores Autonomos de la Industria to affiliate to that Institution the members of the cooperatives associated with Caja Laboral Popular of Mondragón, as from 1st January of the current year"*.

The amount which it was decided to contribute was the minimum established by the Mutualidad, which was 11% of 2,500 pesetas = 275 pesetas a month.

This basis for contributions accounted for approximately 40% of average wages - then at wage grade 1.40 -. This justifiably meant that the complementary part pertaining to the Welfare Service, today Lagun-Aro, being 60%.

In any case 35 years of contributions were necessary to reach the maximum limits in the Mutualidad de Autonomos, and 30 in the complementary Welfare Service created by the Cooperative Group.

However, in 1973, after it had been operating for three years as a Mutua de Prevision Social (Social Welfare Friendly Society) and had been turned into a Industrial Service Cooperative, further studies were carried out on the cover necessary, introducing new variations which shape the essential and complete welfare nature of Lagun-Aro today.

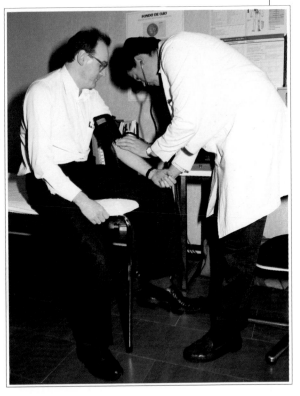

Preventive medicine, a determining factor in the quality of life.

During this adaptation phase the following reforms were carried out:

a) The Internal Regulations of the cooperative were drawn up, excluding the authorised activities, the bodies of the cooperative and dissolution, and in general all concepts which had been established previously in the approved and registered Statutes.

b) Lagun-Aro's specific disciplinary system was adopted, with attention paid to the singular nature of a service and social cover body and, above all, its investment policy, profitability were developed and its financial reserves brought into account.

c) The capitalization and pro rata benefits were adapted, now that they depended on wages, so that they were proportional to the particular income of each member, instead of as from 1967 up to then, equal and minimum, equivalent to wage grade 1, for all members.

d) Pensions were approved for female members on whose deaths surviving husbands would receive a widower's benefit.

e) Benefits were to be revalued every year by 5%, whatever the rate of inflation.

f) The wording was systematically perfected, contributing effectively to its understanding and providing a document which has practically lasted, with little variation, until today.

This system, approved in the General Assembly of the Second Degree Industrial Services Cooperative on 20th April 1974, basically has the following attributes:

a) The contributions are established in direct proportion to the rights to services acquired by each member, measured in terms of temporary and life annuity benefits.

b) Solidarity is the predominant note in the temporary benefits, which are attenuated by individual effort and the working community; at the end of the year, members have no outstanding debts.

c) The system of capitalization created to finance retirement, widowhood and orphanage accumulates the reserves necessary to guarantee the contractually assured benefits, and takes into account the profitability required by actuarial calculations, biometric factors and the progressive revaluation of pensions on the basis of a continued increase in the cost of living.

d) The benefits financed by the capitalization system: retirement, widowhood and orphanage are obtained from a fixed benefit, through the Mutualidad de Autonomos, which covers about 40% of the average income of the cooperators. It is complemented by a pension established by Lagun-Aro which is equivalent to, if contributions have been paid over the full thirty year period, to 60% of wages not including bonus payments.

The calculations mean that whilst those on the lowest income will receive, on retirement, a sum equivalent to at least 100% of their working wage, the same does not happen with those on higher incomes, especially those with wage scales above 2, because the constant sum of the Mutualidad de Autonomos drops from 40% for wage scale 1.4, to 15-20% for the highest paid cooperators.

The contribution in 1990 rose to 15.35%, guaranteeing for a full contribution period of thirty years, 60% of the average wage of the last 10 years.

The percentage indicated, 15.35%, includes the contribution for the annual pension revaluation.

The system still pursues the aim of transparency in the establishment of benefits and contributions, in tune with the possibilities of economically managing the cooperatives; it takes into account the positive development of the State Social Security System which gives increasing cover to workers, and the social control strictly established through the twelve representatives authorised to supervise the management team and administer the general policies of Lagun- Aro from the Governing Council.

4.3 THE WELFARE SERVICE BECOMES INDEPENDENT FROM CLP

In a state of greater calm, the following factors all contributed to the decision for the Mutual Society to break away, as after nine years, it was still legally part of Caja Laboral Popular: firstly, the experience acquired, secondly, the number of companies affiliated (giving a total of 5,161 members in 1967) and lastly, the application of good sense, a product of progressively gaining more knowledge on mutualism.

On 19th June 1969 the Mutua de Previsión Social (Mutual Society for Social Welfare) was constituted by the Director General of the Ministry of Work. This entity was the instrument which definitively established the legal and financial autonomy of Lagun-Aro.

But the creation of the Mutua was not enough, because amongst other reasons to be able to administer autonomously benefits derived from Occupational Accidents and Illnesses it was necessary to be a company, reach an express agreement with Social Security and have a staff of at least 500 workers.

For this reason it was necessary for Lagun-Aro to be associated with Caja Laboral Popular, for which it necessarily had to be a cooperative. Steps were immediately taken on the basis of conventional statutes, with generic references in the authorised activities and the economic structure and Lagun- Aro, S. Coop. Industrial de Segundo Grado (Second Degree Industrial Cooperative) was created on 30th November 1973.

The General Assembly was made up of members of the cooperatives which formed part of the second degree cooperative. As a company Lagun-Aro could opt to cover Occupational Accident and Illness benefits.

However, another year was necessary to resolve finally the complexities of covering the benefit derived from Occupational Accidents. The basic argument had its support in the fact that the Mutualidad de Autonomos to which the cooperatives were affiliated already covered these benefits whether for reasons which originated outside work or for some other natural reason.

On 18th October 1974, contrary to what had been maintained up to then, the Director General for Social Welfare accepted that there was cover through affiliation to the Mutualidad de Autonomos and this definitively settled a subject which had been a real nightmare for almost 15 years every time there was a serious accident or an inspection, routine or not, by the Ministry of Work.

Surprisingly the request made to the Director General for Social Security *"for authorization for Lagun-Aro to assume directly cover of sick leave contingencies derived from occupational accidents or illness"* ...was refused because... *"it is not admissible...as the various cooperatives are included in the Special System for the Self Employed"*...

This was the culmination of a process of adaptation of Lagun-Aro's private System to that established by the State through Social Security. In the end our model had found its legal framework.

The general circumstances which modified the basis of general State policy especially from 1975 on and after the Statute of Autonomy for the Basque Country was approved in 1979, meant that friendly societies came under the responsibility of the Regional Government.

On 3rd September 1987 Lagun-Aro became an Entidad de Previsión Voluntaria (Voluntary Welfare Entity) with its statutes remaining practically the same as those which had been in force for the Second Degree Cooperative since 1973.

27 years had gone by since Lagun-Aro started life on 1st October 1959 as the "social section" of Caja Laboral Popular.

4.4 LAGUN-ARO IN 1990

Bringing to mind conceptualised events from the history of Lagun-Aro teaches us lessons which go beyond the scope of the friendly society created.

In its creation advantage was taken of an unwonted fact: that the Law forced 320 cooperators to create their own social security cover, offering both temporary and life annuity benefits.

The decision, based on a strict and precise interpretation of cooperators as self-employed workers, exploited the threats and uncertainty hanging over it to establish a system in harmony with the condition of cooperators obliged to make the best possible use of resources generated by their companies. It was understood that the contributions to be paid to Social Security were a company cost, like any other. There was a move away from the idea of the protective State,

Main hall of the Head Offices.

on which any form of guile could be practised, in a framework of general acceptance, to obtain benefits of a general social nature almost akin to charity.

Different levels of responsibility were established, based on a prudential balance: members to their cooperatives; cooperatives to the working communities formed by various cooperatives in the area and the communities to the Mutua as a whole.

The different levels of decision are comparable to the overall effort achieving harmony and a balance of interests.

4.5 EMPLOYMENT AID

This benefit has been subject to a continuous process of adaptation as a consequence of the cooperative nature of the labour it attempts to support and of the capacity to take decisions on a community level involving all members, in situations of crisis and restructuring, which, in the last analysis, are the cause of unemployment.

On the other hand, increases in the workforce, based on a sound industrial performance, were excellent: 15.7% annually between 1965 and 1970; 9.5% between 1970 and 1975 and

5.1% between 1975 and 1980. These increases counselled that staffing problems should be solved more by means of internal changes, taking on new activities to achieve full employment or, as was done from 1983 on, establishing intercooperative collaboration consisting of transferring excess staff from cooperatives where there was no demand to those which had created need. This process is known as "relocation". In short, it was a matter of rejecting conventional solutions, which are always expensive, never satisfactory and very complex, in order to identify the situations which really merit aid from collective contributions.

Hence this system of cover was called *"Employment Aid"*.

The start of the study of the regulations for this benefit date back to 1978. The specific regulations were very cautious in their stipulations, requiring that before this benefit could be drawn there should be a qualification period, based on a prior report, to assess the situation on the basis of certain factors in order to be able to adopt precisely the right solution.

Almost all the determining factors have subsequently been maintained, but whereas at the start the benefits consisted of interest free loans which later had to be repaid, now the aid is conclusive and does not have to be repaid.

"Employment Aid" became more complex, especially when the alternative **relocation** process prior to direct unemployment benefit was established.

It includes the following aid:

a) **Relocation expenses:** travel, subsistence and differences in wage grade.

b) **Unemployment:** a direct benefit for an **unemployed** person, if relocation is impossible.

c) **Early retirement:** for cooperatives with structural unemployment, if the member is over 58 and difficult to relocate.

d) **Indemnity:** under the same conditions as early retirement, but if the member were under 58.

e) **Professional retraining:** as a cover complementary to the aid given by Government and other bodies.

At critical moments, such as the first half of the eighties, this benefit was very controversial because it always seemed insufficient for those needing it whilst it was regarded as burden by those who did not. Anyhow, in general terms, its creation was very educational for a limited social group who had to face up to an unfamiliar situation for which it was not mentally prepared.

But if the cooperatives as a whole suffered, the members involved suffered more. Their having to travel to another cooperative, day after day, and the partial loss of income were probably, in their niggardliness, the most expressive differentiating factor between employed workers and cooperative members.

There was a spontaneous comparison at this time with other local companies suffering from the same problems. It was seen that the formulas offered by the General Social Security System supported by the national budget were more generous and more lax in their application. The fact was that the

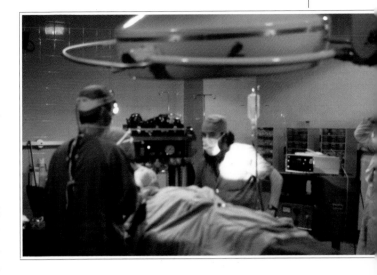

Medical care.

contributions paid to Lagun-Aro by the cooperatives only amounted to a third of those paid by other companies, because the aim was, by calling on the responsibility of the Group and on internal economies, to reduce costs to increase efficiency in competitive terms.

In these circumstances there was a certain amount of deviation in the contracting of non-members, under the protection of the regulations making the work force more flexible, which is treated with tolerance in the Spanish Law on Cooperatives and which protected by the greater cover of the (state) unemployment benefit provided room for manoeuvre for certain cooperatives in the Group.

On the other hand, the Decree of 19th June 1985 enabled unemployment to be capitalized in a single payment to be used to pay capital contributions to companies, a fact which has permitted new members to make the compulsory capital contribution required by all the cooperatives.

This situation, now perfectly under control, meant that the number of non-members working in cooperatives approached 10% of the total work force. This fact, although not strictly ideal - in terms of the basic internal principles of the Group - represents the balance which has been reached between aspiring members in their prior phase of employed worker. It also easily complies with the legally established limits and offers room for manoeuvre in the face of the fickleness of demand, even though it does not fully comply with **Basic Principle 3 - Sovereignty of Labour** which advocates *"renouncing the systematic contracting of salaried workers"*.

In 1990, with a contribution of 2.5% of wages the volume of financing totalled 950 million pesetas and as of 31st December the following aid had been given:

– 17 definitive relocations

– 262 early retirements

– 3 indemnified "early retirements"

– 237 temporary relocations leaving only 20 members, who could functionally be assigned other jobs, unemployed.

This benefit is one which was not considered or admitted when the Welfare Service began. This service, in spite of its weak economic impact, has been an imaginative example of solidarity.

GENERAL ORGANISATIONAL CHART OF LAGUN-ARO

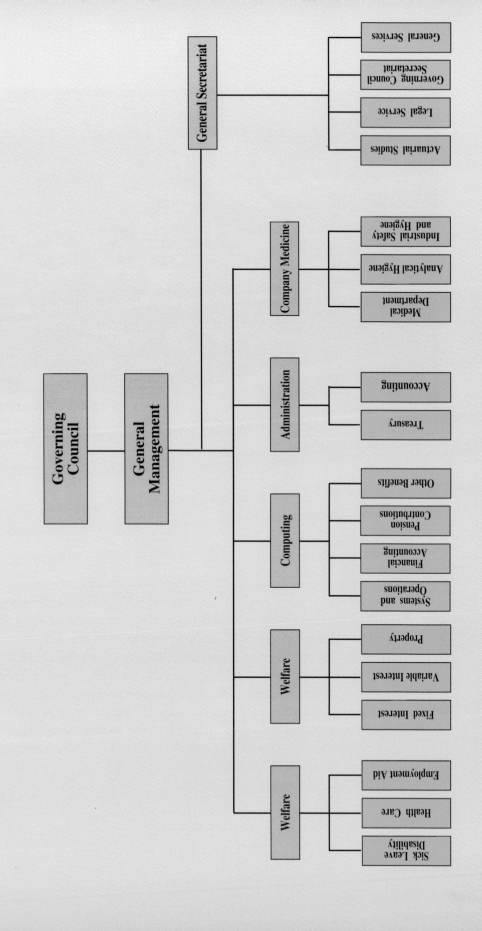

Governing Council

General Management

General Secretariat
- Actuarial Studies
- Legal Service
- Governing Council Secretariat
- General Services

Company Medicine
- Medical Department
- Analytical Hygiene
- Industrial Safety and Hygiene

Administration
- Treasury
- Accounting

Computing
- Systems and Operations
- Financial Accounting
- Pension Contributions
- Other Benefits

Welfare
- Fixed Interest
- Variable Interest
- Property

Welfare
- Sick Leave Disability
- Health Care
- Employment Aid

Eskola Politeknikoa, Lagun Aro, Ikerlan and Caja Laboral Popular with the Fagor industrial complex in the background.

"**F**or companies to achieve their social and economic aims, they must be governed by the principle of efficiency. It is essential for companies to establish at their core a nucleus of responsibilities in order to develop specific missions to obtain a product or service. This means that at the heart of a company there is a creative and homogenising force which is capable of conceiving the task, gathering together and organising the means necessary, etc., so that the modern techniques of organisation of work, rationalisation, etc., are permanently up to date, because economic activity designed to achieve production is not something spontaneous, but is the consequence of a process of transformation, which is more complex every day given the progress of technology"
J. Mª Arizmendiarrieta)

5. THE INDUSTRIAL AND SERVICES GROUP

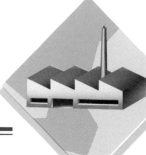

The development of the GROUP over thirty years objectively shows how it has gone through very distinct periods.

- **The first from 1961 to 1980**, approximately, was really a period of expansion supported by the policy of creation of cooperatives which speeded up in this period thanks, on the one hand, to the favourable circumstances in the western world and, on the other, to the fact that the cooperatives knew how to make the most of an internal market made more accessible by the protectionist measures imposed by the Franco dictatorship. Average net profits totalled 7.6% over sales and employment growth maintained an annual rate of 10%.

The second from 1980 to 1990. On the threshold of this period, in 1979, there was for the second time an unforeseen and disproportionate increase in the price of fuel. The need to tackle the overseas market resolutely meant that costs had to reduced to be competitive, which was done with great difficulty, by means of technological innovations. It was also a period in which Management also had to be prepared for a new international confrontation. In 1986, with Spain finally joining the European Economic Community, a completely new stage was set before us which had to be trodden with the backing of resources coherent with its size. Profits were not high, close to 0.5% over sales, and employment only rose by an annual rate of 2.1%.

- **A third phase** can be spoken of, within, yet at the same time separate from the last decade, beginning in 1985 and lasting until 1990, in which, once an enormous effort had been made to adapt, positive results began to be obtained and there was net growth in employment, but in relative terms, scarcely totalling 50% of the figures achieved over the first twenty years of the Experience. Profitability returned, with a figure of 4.5% over sales.

The information which follows is so telling that further comment is unncesessary, although the evidence clearly demonstrates that the Cooperatives in the Group are vulnerable to the macroeconomic development occurring within the broad framework of its activities.

5.1 STATISTICS: 1966 TO 1990

in millions of pesetas

Years	Sales	Exports	No. of workers MSG as of 31.12	No. of workers ISG as of 31.12	Investment	Profit
1966	2,892	52	4,866	4,796	409	238
1967	3,606	101	5,161	5,067	461	258
1968	4,169	336	6,048	5,924	572	266
1969	6,348	503	8,081	7,928	787	550
1970	7,059	786	8,743	8,543	992	494
1971	8,164	1,043	9,650	9,461	797	302
1972	10,676	1,291	10,493	10,218	729	853
1973	13,206	1,618	11,597	11,260	1,292	1,333
1974	17,693	1,918	13,310	12,911	2,362	1,405
1975	19,694	2,347	13,808	13,189	2,851	1,442
1976	24,833	3,117	15,417	14,510	3,579	2,056
1977	34,119	4,309	16,504	15,716	4,003	2,322
1978	43,753	5,837	17,022	15,923	3,671	2,138
1979	57,189	9,040	18,295	16,814	4,638	1,507
1980	69,064	13,576	17,733	17,424	4,844	517
1981	84,962	19,766	18,461	17,238	5,257	-884
1982	96,871	21,316	18,788	17,387	4,123	256
1983	110,293	24,080	18,744	17,133	5,353	854
1984	121,190	28,192	18,795	16,918	7,132	-2,387
1985	140,020	31,899	19,161	17,176	9,208	-263
1986	158,923	33,008	19,669	17,514	11,058	4,239
1987	179,345	35,718	20,409	18,262	12,169	8,950
1988	206,339	41,157	21,204	19,150	14,824	11,317
1989	253,088	47,220	21,928	20,157	21,084	11,569
1990	299,231	54,808	22,860	21,089	26,268	13,438

 *t different times, the circumstances of the social climate produced different ways of creating cooperatives"*

a) Sales

The sales performance of the Cooperatives over the last 25 years is shown in the following graph:

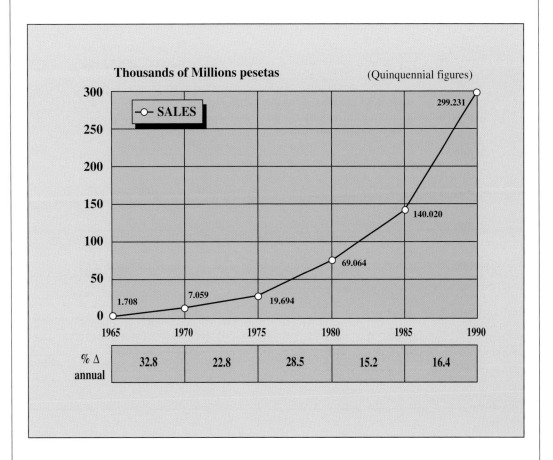

Thousands of Millions pesetas   (Quinquennial figures)

% Δ annual	32.8	22.8	28.5	15.2	16.4

The quinquennial growth in turnover has been ever greater in absolute terms for, mainly, two reasons. On the one hand, the gradual increase in the number of cooperatives in the Group and, on the other, as they are figures in current pesetas, the impact of inflation is especially notable in the periods most affected. However, the percentage increases in sales have gradually slowed down - except for the sudden rise in the period 1975/1980 -, which stands to reason bearing in mind that the starting point is ever higher.

b) Exports

For their part, over the last 25 years the export figures were as follows:

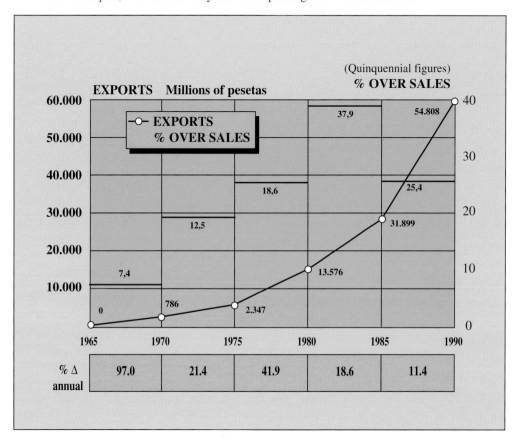

The first sales were made to the overseas market in 1966. From then on, this variable has accelerated faster than total sales, except during the last five-year period, in which the average annual increase in exports was 11.4% compared with a growth of 16.4% in total turnover. The gradual downward slide of the dollar, the problems experienced by Latin American countries and the recovery of internal demand which has eased the export endeavour, have all had their effect. The share of exports in total sales has gradually increased, totalling nearly 21% (31% if Eroski's sales are not taken in account), a percentage which is representative of performance over the last two five-year periods.

c) Jobs

The workforces of the Cooperatives in the Mondragon Cooperative Group have developed as shown in the following graph:

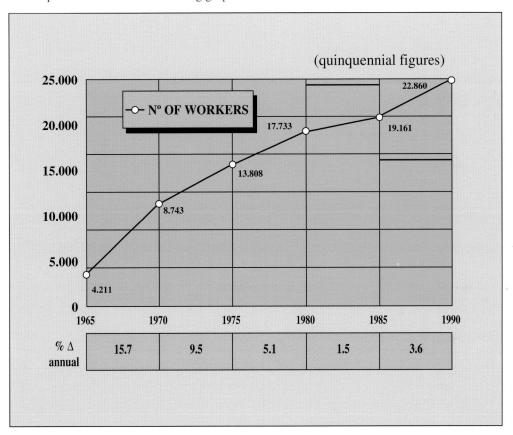

After the stagnation in the creation of jobs in the first half of the eighties, in which the annual increase was only 1.5%, in recent years the generation of employment has in part regained its rhythm, although it is still far from the levels achieved in the first three five-year periods of the Experience. The graph shows two clearly different periods, whose point of inflection is to be found in the year 1978. Prior to that year, the growth in the workforce of the Mondragon Cooperative Group had maintained an accelerated rate, 13.2% annually in cumulative terms over the period 64/75. However, subsequent to 1978 the growth rate dropped to a cautious annual average of 2.2%.

d) Investment

The renewal of equipment on the part of the Mondragon Cooperative Group occurred at the rate shown below:

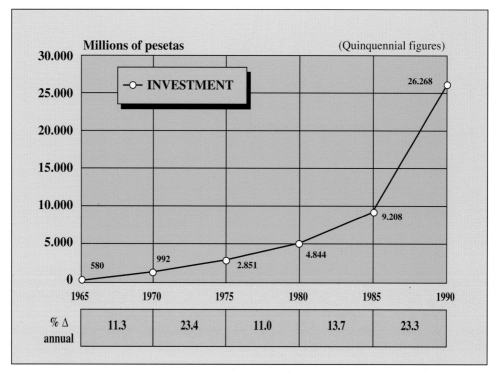

The investments carried out by the Cooperatives experienced marked annual percentage increases during the first two five- year periods. Subsequently the recession suffered during the late seventies and early eighties led to a limited generation of cashflow and, consequently, to a weakening in the level of financial independence, forcing the cooperatives to be more prudent in their investment policies. On the other hand, the last five-year period 1985/90 has been characterised by a more expansive market, with a 5% growth in demand for consumer goods and 15% for capital goods. In tune with the economic situation, and also propitiated by the recent reconversion and relaunching plans for the Group, there has been a strong renewal of production equipment, which has enabled costs to be reduced and capacity per production unit to be increased.

e) Profits

The profits made by the Cooperatives and the corresponding profitability over sales have developed in the following way over the last 25 years.

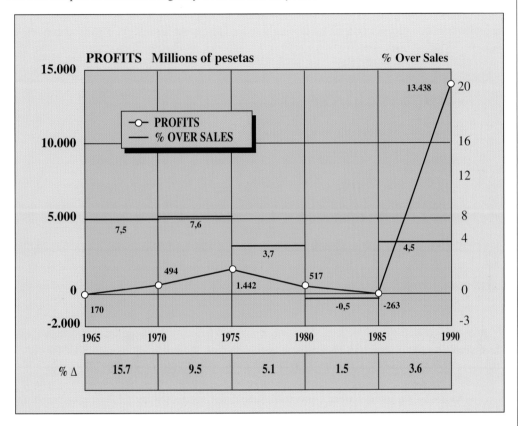

The profits achieved by the Cooperatives of the Industrial and Services Group were positive until 1979, when they subsequently slumped to negative levels, with the lowest figure corresponding to 1984 with 2,387 million pesetas in losses. Profitability over sales stayed above 7.5% during the first two five year periods, dropping to -0.5% in the period 1979/85 and then recovering in the last few years, to reach 4.5% in the period 1985/90. This was due mainly to the economic climate which in its main variables has driven consumption and investment with an average growth of 5% in GDP.

5.2 THE CREATION OF COOPERATIVES

At different times, the circumstances of the social climate produced different ways of creating cooperatives.

In the same way their association with CLP, the only vehicle of integration for the incipient Group, adopted criteria increasingly more in keeping with legal, financial and social rules.

a) 1959 (Foundation of CLP) to 1963

The associated cooperatives at this time were:

Arrasate:	01.10.59	Urssa:	01.10.61
Funcor:	01.10.59	Lana:	01.01.62
Ulgor:	01.10.59	Vicon:	16.09.63

This was the period in which CLP was created. On 1.10.59 our entity was founded by three cooperatives. The San José Consumer Cooperative, also a founder, is not listed as it was taken over by Eroski in 1971.

This small bit of history was full of stutterings. It was the period when URSSA of Vitoria was created by people from Mondragon, by assimilating the legal formula which Ulgor had adopted with success, and Vicon was set up in San Sebastian by members of HOAC (a Workers Organisation run by the Catholic Church), also based on the Mondragon model.

As far as the others were concerned, Lana was supported by CLP in its overall and financial management, and was provided with an initial injection of capital which consisted in equalling the volume of capital constituted by its own members.

"30 cooperatives were created over fourteen years (1972-1985), giving standing to the model for generating employment followed, by means of establishing activities in the places where Caja Laboral Popular was attracting people's savings".

b) 1964 to 1971

The association of cooperatives became more general, with the following new members:

Soraluce:	13.11.63	Tolsan:	01.07.68
Copreci:	02.03.64	Goiti:	09.12.68
Ederlan:	06.03.64	Alkargo:	11.02.69
Ulma:	21.05.64	OchandianoT.:	07.08.69
Guría Ind.:	14.07.64	Batz:	01.10.69
Irizar:	14.07.64	Covimar:	15.10.69
Miba:	14.07.64	Biurrarena:	30.10.69
Matrici:	17.07.65	Eredu:	21.11.69
Fagor Electr.:	02.01.66	Matz-Erreka:	29.11.69
Goizper:	17.02.66	Egurko:	11.12.69
Tajo:	17.02.66	Elkar:	22.12.69
Impreci:	19.07.67	Eroski:	01.01.70
Danobat:	08.02.68	Zubiola:	19.02.70
Amat:	01.07.68	Auzo-Lagun:	05.05.70
Ampo:	01.07.68	Coinalde:	03.03.71
Coinma:	01.07.68	Danona Lt.:	12.04.71
Danona:	01.07.68	Alecop:	07.06.71
Enara:	01.07.68	Orbea:	27.12.71
Orona:	01.07.68		

This list of 37 cooperatives includes various models for start-ups which we shall try to summarise, grouping them under different headings:

* Created by means of a CLP promotion contract

The following belong to this model: Lana, Soraluce, Copreci, Ederlan, Auzo-Lagun and Alecop. The contract formally signed with Soraluce, Copreci and Ederlan, equivalent to that agreed with Lana, basically had the following characteristics:

a) It was set in a framework of solidarity, tending towards the creation of an organism (Group) of a higher level in which certain more complex management functions would be carried out.

b) The Caja determined the technical and economic means necessary, intervening in the appointment of management staff.

c) The Managing Director of Caja Laboral became Managing Director of the Cooperative.

d) The Cooperative accepted 20% of the capital necessary from CLP, in the capacity of sleeping partner.

e) The cooperative would pay CLP all expenses incurred, and 5% of the increase in profits obtained each year compared with the last.

* Conversion of limited companies

In this period of 7 years, crises were suffered by industries in different periods of economic adjustment in which a new model of behaviour was imposed, which was undoubtedly international. Industries were also hit by cycles which were establishing greater severity and were urging the employment of greater intellectual potential and a necessary spirit of innovation.

The following became cooperatives through this system: Irizar, Danobat, Coinma, Enara (Gaitu, when it joined) and Orbea. For some of these companies the conversion was not easy and it became evident that financial and management support was required because (as was demonstrated later, on so many occasions) the change in their legal structure was not sufficient to strengthen their weakened financial structure and unfortunate performance.

* Mergers and splits

The merger carried out by several consumer cooperatives to form Eroski is significant. As a result the following, which were associated with Caja Laboral disappeared, forming with some others, the basis for Eroski: San José, Andra-Mari, La Maquinesa, La Guerniquesa and La Zornozana.

Fagor Electrotécnica was also created as a split from Ulgor, nine years after having been established as a Division of that cooperative in 1957.

* Independent creation

Of the 37 cooperatives associated during this period, 23 followed this model. They used the statutes already in force in the Mondragon Cooperatives, but did not require the direct intervention of Caja Laboral Popular. A clearer indication of the model followed is the fact that they did not become associated with Caja Laboral until several years later, by means of the drawing up of the appropriate dossier which, on several occasions, was at first rejected (the case of Goiti, for example).

c) 1972 to 1985

The Cooperatives of the Mondragon Cooperative Group which became associated with Caja Laboral Popular during this period were:

Embega:	18.01.72	Uraldi:	19.06.80
Cikautxo:	21.01.72	Maiak:	09.07.80
Doiki:	24.03.73	Urola:	14.05.80
Fagor Ind.:	18.02.74	Barrenetxe:	12.09.80
Maier:	01.10.74	Oiarso:	08.01.80
Eika:	11.10.74	Osatu:	29.01.81
RPK:	08.11.74	Gogar:	19.02.81
Gaiko:	05.12.74	Oihana:	02.06.81
Lealde:	10.12.74	Guría O.P.:	30.06.81
Bertako:	02.04.75	Aurki:	01.01.82
Ortza:	02.04.75	Ikerlan:	20.05.82
Sakana:	14.06.76	Lenniz:	09.07.82
Ederfil:	17.11.76	Ondoan:	15.07.82
Kendu:	10.01.77	Orkli:	30.07.82
Aurrenak:	30.03.77	Cos. Alaveses:	24.01.83
Zertan:	19.10.77	Bihar:	24.03.83
Latz:	30.10.77	Leunkor:	05.04.83
Dikar:	13.12.77	Uldata:	21.06.83
Kide:	15.11.78	Etorki:	12.07.84
Herriola:	05.01.79	Fagor Clima:	13.07.84
Ona-pres:	09.01.79	Behi-Alde:	11.09.84
Txurtxil:	13.03.79	Matriplast:	03.10.84
Lan-Mobel:	04.05.79	Leroa:	17.10.84
Hertell:	29.06.79	Artxa:	29.10.84
Radar:	18.07.79	Oinakar:	14.11.84
Izarraitz:	06.10.79		

During this period, the model for creating cooperatives was characterised by the following:

* Splits or creation from within other cooperatives

Fagor Industrial, Leunkor and Fagor Clima were created as splits from Ulgor; Lenniz,

Uldata (now not existing under that name), Radar and Aurki can be considered as new promotions within the Fagor Cooperative Group.

From Matrici, Matriplast was born and from the Nerbion Group, Ondoan.

* Independent creation

Several cooperatives were created under different circumstances, sometimes at the request of the workers in order to maintain their jobs, such as in the cases of Txurtxil, Ona-Pres and Maiak and at other times simply following the general statutes of the Group, as in the cases of Lan-Mobel, Hertell and Aurrenak. Overall, seven or eight cooperatives were created at this time with the common denominator that a certain amount of time went by from their birth as cooperatives to their association with Caja Laboral Popular.

* Direct creation from CLP

30 cooperatives were created over these 14 years (1972-1985) following the model for generation of employment, through the idea of establishing activities where Caja Laboral Popular was attracting savings. Their creation was promoted by the Business Division as part of the new conception of its functions adopted precisely at this time, 1969-70.

There were a large number of cooperatives created, which means that they cannot all be described, but the first were Cikautxo, Doiki, Embega, Maier, Eika and RPK.

d) 1986-1990

During this period the creation of cooperatives has practically ground to a halt.

Only the following were created:

Artalde:	17.02.86	MSE:	18.01.88
Olarri:	25.02.86	Diara:	31.05.88
Berriola:	01.03.86	Audilan:	27.12.90
		Udala:	28.12.90

It is therefore quite easy to describe the methods followed for their creation:

Artalde, a sheep rearing and agricultural cooperative, drew up its Viability Plan through the Agrofood Promotion Area, supported by Eroski.

Olarri, was the result of the break-away from Goiti of its construction section.

Berriola, was created by the merger of Gaztelu and Ekain.

Maier Servicios Electrónicos (MSE), was created in Munguía to take the place of Munko, which had disappeared. It is, in effect, the only industrial cooperative which has been created and has joined the Group in the last three years.

Diara was created with the support of Eskola Politeknikoa and the Business Division of CLP in search of professionals in industrial design, in order to make this singularly necessary contribution to the Group.

Audilan arose from the separation of the Auditing Department of the Business Division of CLP, in response to the Law of 12th July 1988 on Account Auditing.

Udala was created when Lana's dairy product division broke away.

e) Conclusions

Of the 99 worker cooperatives which make up the list of those associated with CLP, 45% were created directly through the Business Division, although until 1970 a more precarious and spontaneous model was followed as the Business Division did not exist in its ultimate form. More attention was paid to their geographical location, with the corresponding Viability Studies carried out and action being taken with a view to forming Cooperative Groups based on the local model.

Consequently, the direction taken for the promotion of the Group could be said to be as follows:

a) Caja Laboral Popular's vocation for the creation of employment has been necessary for the Mondragon Cooperative Group to achieve its current level of importance.

b) Spontaneous outbursts of the independent creation of cooperatives have been totally reduced as a consequence of the greater difficulties of achieving success, in business terms and, probably due to the cultural change implied in the little attraction which being a worker, member and owner of a company merits.

c) Strictly speaking, in the last five years, only three new cooperatives have been created from CLP and the Group in our geographical area. On the other hand, several companies were wound up as a result of the crisis suffered from 1974 to 1985: Ikus XXI, Aneko, Citamare, Dormicoop, Gogar, Labeko and more recently Basarko, Munko and MSE. However, there has been a marked growth in employment, especially in Service cooperatives, with the creation of close to 3,700 jobs.

5.3 THE CREATION OF THE GROUP

In the origins of cooperative experience, one man, Don José María Arizmendiarrieta, was first to interpret the virtues of work as an indispensable factor for achieving social well-being.

He was conscious of the limitations of the natural wealth of the Basque Country and always believed that the capacity of its men and women for work was its most promising and almost only asset, to compensate for the lack of goods in this small, not very generous country.

He appealed to the consciences of the business men he knew, urging them to change their business behaviour which paid little respect to the uncertain future which was approaching. He also appealed to them to change the model of social relations as he wanted workers to be able to participate in company decisions.

Based on these assumptions and having realised in time that the businessmen of the golden era of protectionism were making mistakes, and trying to harmonise the eternal dialectic tension between capital and labour, he encouraged the creation of the first cooperatives.

a) The birth of the cooperatives

It was not until 1959 that the factory in Vitoria (see chapter 1), at that time Talleres Ulgor, was transformed from an individual company into a cooperative, as a result of steps taken by the Ministry of Work on 3rd April that year.

Cooperatives were born therefore, everywhere, in spontaneous succession. They survived 12 years of recession (1974 to 1985) and in 1990, with 99 associated with the Group, they have a turnover of close to 300,000 million pesetas. They provide employment for almost 23,000 people and will have a cashflow this year of practically 24,000 million pesetas, without taking into account the profitability of the technical reserves of Lagun-Aro, - as strictly speaking these are external funds linked to obligations contracted with Lagun-Aro's members -, nor those of Caja Laboral Popular.

In these thirty-five long years, a group of more than one hundred industrial cooperatives has been created, whose main aims were originally:

a) The creation of wealth through community work based on cooperative norms and principles, as a genuine means, rooted in the Basque Country, of maintaining social well-being.

b) A basic uninterrupted commitment to make possible, day by day, the rebirth and adaptation of this social experience.

GENERAL ORGANISATIONAL CHART OF THE MONDRAGON COOPERATIVE GROUP (REGIONAL)

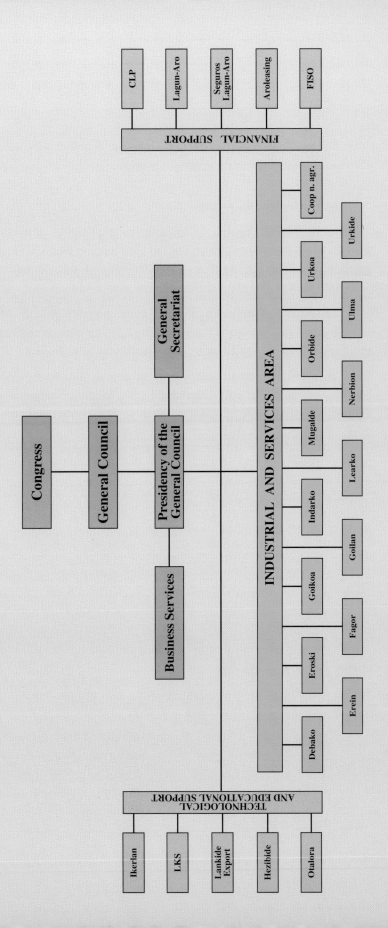

c) The conjunction of productive and service activities with financial and social ones, to make such a social experience possible, harmoniously.

b) The birth of the Groups

From 1964 on, between the cooperatives in the Group, there was a movement towards providing mutual support which, in the following decades was to acquire progressive importance, becoming the basic suuport of the business policy of the Mondragon Cooperative Group (GCM).

This drive to form groups, started by the cooperatives in the Mondragón area, was to take fifteen years to spread to other local areas. If we exclude the Fagor Group, the relative novelty and recent consolidation of these structures is quite evident.

There follows a description, in order of their creation, of the Cooperative Groups which exist today in the GCM, with some basic figures for their configuration up to 31st December 1990 and some business variables showing the size and features of each of them.

rom 1964 on, between the cooperatives in the Group, there was a movement towards providing mutual support which, in the following decades was to acquire progressive importance, becoming the basic support of the business policy of the Mondragon Cooperative Group (GCM)."

FAGOR, Flagship of the Cooperative Experience in the industrial sector.

1) FAGOR (1964)

(Cooperatives which make up the Group: Copreci, Fabrelec, Fagor Arrasate, Fagor Automation, Fagor Clima, Fagor Ederlan, Fagor Electrodomesticos, Fagor Electronica, Fagor Industrial, Fagor Leunkor, Fagor Minidomesticos, Fagor Mueble, Fagor Sistemas, Luzuriaga)

The current Fagor Group has its origins in the creation of the Ularco Industrial Complex in 1964, by means of the grouping of the cooperatives then located in the Leniz Valley, in order to provide them with common services, to take advantage of economies of scale and to create a strong business unit.

In 1975, the Complex became the Ularco Group and in 1986, making use of its most well known trademark, it changed its name to the Fagor Group.

The Central Departments of Fagor are now quite large, employing the services of 90 members. Internal regulations and remuneration have been standardised and 100% of the profits set aside for returns are pooled.

FORECAST HIGHLIGHTS FOR THE GROUP AS OF 31.12.1990	
Sales:	106,050 Mptas.
Exports/sales:	25.65%
Net profit:	3,577 Mptas.
Workforce:	7,331
% of profits set aside for returns which are pooled:	100

2) GOILAN (1978)

(Cooperatives which make up the Group: Ampo, Ederfil, Eredu, Irizar, Kendu, Orkli)

This Group was created with the aim of providing the cooperatives in the Goiherri area, with services in common enabling them to reduce costs, achieve more efficient management and consolidate the base cooperatives.

With time, consolidation has progressively gained importance as an aim of the Group in relation to the centralisation of services, whilst these have maintained the structure drawn up initially.

EREDU S. Coop.
in Legorreta, Guipúzcoa

FORECAST HIGHLIGHTS FOR THE GROUP AS OF 31.12.1990	
Sales:	13,942 Mptas.
Exports/sales:	43.80 %
Net profit:	491 M ptas.
Workforce:	1,025
% of profits set aside for returns which are pooled:	70

3) ORBIDE (1978)

(Cooperatives which make up the Group: Berriola, Guria Industrias, Latz, Orona, Vicon)

The Orbide Group was created in 1978 to associate the Cooperatives located in the River Oria and River Bidasoa areas, providing them with services in common and strengthening their consolidation as companies.

In 1986, in order to include four more Cooperatives in the Group, which already had six, Orbide was divided into two groups, Orbide and Murgalde, with the cooperatives located in the Oria and San Sebastian areas remaining in the first group.

This Group, widely dispersed in sectorial terms, has maintained, as an essential activity, Central Services, which once they were redistributed after the division of the previous Orbide Group, have remained largely unchanged.

The dome of the Palau Sant Jordi (Sports Arena) during construction.

FORECAST HIGHLIGHTS FOR THE GROUP AS OF 31.12.1990

Sales:	8,792 Mptas.
Exports/sales:	5.90 %
Net profit:	381 Mptas.
Workforce:	915
% of profits set aside for returns which are pooled:	0

CIKAUTXO factory on the Berriatua industrial estate.

4) LEARKO (1979)

(Cooperatives which make up the Group: Cikautxo, Eika, Herriola, Kide, Lealde)

In 1974, as a response to a worrying situation, the Business Division of Caja Laboral carried out an analysis of the socio-economic situation of the Lea-Artibai area. This study indicated that there was an urgent need to relaunch businesses, which on the basis of the cooperative system, would enable the area to develop.

In consequence, after the creation of cooperatives in the area, the Learko Group was created in 1979. Its Central Services progressively acquired the necessary structure and by 1982 the organisational framework was fully established.

From 1982 notable advances have been made in terms of consolidating intercooperative solidarity, by means of standardising regulations and remuneration systems and progressively increasing the percentage of profits pooled by the Cooperatives.

FORECAST HIGHLIGHTS FOR THE GROUP AS OF 31.12.1990

Sales:	6,883 Mptas.
Exports/sales:	36.80 %
Net profit:	254 Mptas.
Workforce:	587
% of profits set aside for returns which are pooled:	70

5) DEBAKO (1981)

(Cooperatives which make up the Group: Danobat, Goiti, Izarraitz, Soraluce, Txurtxil)

This Group was created in 1981 to group together, on a sectorial basis, the GCM cooperatives in the machine tool sector. In 1982 there was a change of direction, with sectorial criteria being replaced by that of location. As a result, the Cooperative Lealde joined the Learko Group, Ona-Pres joined the Nerbion Group and Izarraitz which had been going to join the Urkide Group, finally remained outside the Local Groups set up.

The DANOBAT and GOITI factories in the background with the IDEKO research centre in the foreground.

At present, the Debako Group has firmly reestablished its sectorial vocation, strengthening its relations with the other Cooperatives in the machine tool sector.

The Central Services, which at first had an embryonic structure, underwent a relaunch process from 1983, with the creation of the IDEKO research centre in 1986, to which Lealde and Ona-Pres also belong. At present, Debako is one of the groups which has most clearly defined and applied its sectorial strategy.

FORECAST HIGHLIGHTS FOR THE GROUP AS OF 31.12.1990	
Sales:	10,596 Mptas.
Exports/sales:	33.80 %
Net profit:	363 Mptas.
Workforce:	942
% of profits set aside for returns which are pooled:	70

6) NERBION-IBAIZABAL (1980-1986)

(Cooperatives which make up the Nerbion Group: Bihar, Elkar, Matrici, Matriplast, Ona-Pres, Ondoan) (Cooperatives which make up the Ibaizabal Group: Batz, Covimar, Funcor, Tolsan)

The Nerbion Group was created in 1980 on the basis of mainly geographical criteria, grouping together four cooperatives located in Bilbao and the surrounding area which carried out activities in different sectors.

The Ibaizabal Group was created in 1986, grouping together the cooperatives located on the banks of the River Ibaizabal, in order to centralise certain services and achieve consolidation, by tackling the reconversion processes underway in three of the four cooperatives making up the Group.

This Group has remained in an embryonic state during these years and its standardisation in terms of regulations and remuneration has been seriously hindered by the negative development of the companies.

FORECAST HIGHLIGHTS FOR THE GROUP AS OF 31.12.1990

Sales:	12,108	Mptas.
Exports/sales:	41.40	%
Net profit:	378	Mptas.
Workforce:	1,211	
% of profits set aside for returns which are pooled:		
- Nerbion Group:	5	*
- Ibaizabal Group:	0	

---

* It should be pointed out that the Cooperatives in the Nerbion Group also deduct 20% from their profits set aside for returns, in order to establish a common fund to finance commitments with third parties.

7) URKIDE (1980)

(Cooperatives which make up the Group: Danona, Egurko, Lan-Mobel, Leroa, Zubiola)

This Group was created to group together the cooperatives located in the Azpeitia-Zumaia area, combining local criteria with its sectorial configuration, as it only included cooperatives belonging to two sectors: wood furniture and machine tools to manufacture such furniture.

Once the Group had been created, two more cooperatives joined, Maiak in 1980 and Basarte in 1983. At present Urkide consists of five Cooperatives, in the two aforementioned production sectors.

The initial structure of the central services, with the exception of the disappearance of the Promotion Department, has basically been maintained. However, the communal services of a sectorial nature have been notably strengthened, in the areas of design, product, marketing and exports.

DANONA S. Coop industrial complex, in the Lasao industrial estate, Azpeitia.

FORECAST HIGHLIGHTS FOR THE GROUP AS OF 31.12.1990

Sales:	6,766 Mptas.
Exports/sales:	23.80 %
Net profit:	50 Mptas.
Workforce:	707
% of profits set aside for returns which are pooled:	0

8) INDARKO (1980)

(Cooperatives which make up the Group: Alkargo, Maier, MSE, Uraldi)

In 1980, the cooperatives Alkargo, Maier, Munko and Uraldi, located in Mungia and Gernika, interested in having services in common, created this Group, purely on the basis of their location.

In January 1986 the Group was dissolved due to the serious financial imbalances between the various Cooperatives.

When these imbalances were reduced, Munko closed and MSE created, the cooperatives MSE, Alkargo, Maier and Uraldi proceeded to relaunch Indarko, appointing a Managing Director and maintaining its Local Group character, although the new activities started are intimately related with the existing ones, so that the Group can progressively move towards sectorialization.

FORECAST HIGHLIGHTS FOR THE GROUP AS OF 31.12.1990

Sales:	5,080 Mptas.
Exports/sales:	22.20 %
Net profit:	325 Mptas.
Workforce:	412
% of profits set aside for returns which are pooled:	0

9) EIBARKO-BERELAN (2) (1981-1982)

(Cooperatives which make up the Eibarko Group: Doiki, Orbea, Osatu)

(Cooperatives which make up the Berelan Group: Impreci, Matz-Erreka, Urola)

In 1981 an attempt was made to create the Eibarko Group by associating Cooperatives located in Mallabia and Bérriz. This project remained in a latent state for seven years. In 1988 a Managing Director was named, with responsibility for promoting the consolidation of the Group and the Cooperatives of which it is made up.

Berelan was created in 1982 as a local grouping of Cooperatives located in Bergara (although cooperatives in the Debako and Fagor Groups also have plants in Bergara).

The lack of development of the Berelan group is unanimously attributed to the difficult economic situation of its Cooperatives, which has prevented any advances in their consolidation.

The geographical proximity of both Groups, the need to consolidate their common structures and the strategy of the GCM of establishing local groups with a wider business and social base, mean that Eibarko and Berelan shall progressively draw closer, join together and integrate.

FORECAST HIGHLIGHTS FOR THE GROUP AS OF 31.12.1990

Sales:	**6,000 Mptas.**
Exports/sales:	**12.80 %**
Net profit:	**152 Mptas.**
Workforce:	**546**
% of profits set aside for returns which are pooled:	0

(2) Dikar, Goizper and Olarri have been included in the Berelan Groups for reasons of geographical proximity, although they have not been fully integrated into the Local Group.

10) URCOA (1981)

(Cooperatives which make up the Group: Aurrenak, Coinalde, Coinma, Talleres Ochandiano, Urssa)

On the basis of principally local criteria, the Urcoa Group was created as a Vitoria Cooperative Group, including five cooperatives from the capital of the province of Alava. In 1988 the cooperative Talleres Ochandiano from the province of Vizcaya also joined.

Over these years, the Central Services have maintained a lightweight structure, which could be strengthened shortly. A greater consolidation of the Group is also planned by means of increasing the percentage of profits pooled and by establishing similar wage levels for the Cooperatives which make up the group. The strategy of diversification maintained by the Urcoa Group up to now, is also being subjected to revision.

Night view of AURRENAK S. Coop. in Ali-Gobeo, Vitoria.

FORECAST HIGHLIGHTS FOR THE GROUP AS OF 31.12.1990

Sales:	6,369 Mptas.
Exports/sales:	11.40 %
Net profit:	519 Mptas.
Workforce:	574
% of profits set aside for returns which are pooled:	70

11) ULMA (1983)

(Cooperatives which make up the Group: Enara, Oinakar, Ulma)

The Ulma Group was created with the aim of grouping together, on the basis of their location, the Cooperatives located in the Oñate area. However, from the start Cooperatives such as Lana, Lenniz and Fagor Industrial were excluded, due to their links to the Erein and Fagor Groups.

Over the years, this Group has achieved a significant level of homogenisation in terms of its regulations and of consolidation, having approved a one hundred percent pooling of returns for 1991.

FORECAST HIGHLIGHTS FOR THE GROUP AS OF 31.12.1990

Sales:	12,890 Mptas.
Exports/sales:	16.40 %
Net profit:	1,264 Mptas.
Workforce:	941
% of profits set aside for returns which are pooled:	40.5

12) EREIN (1985)

(Cooperatives which make up the Group: Artalde, Artxa, Barrenetxe, Behi-Alde, Cosecheros Alaveses, Erein Comercial, Etorki, Lana, Miba, Udala)

On the initiative of the Agrofood Promotion Area of the Business Division of Caja Laboral, and after maturing the process for four years, the EREIN Group was created in 1985. It currently includes 8 Cooperatives from the agrofood sector, an indication of its obviously sectorial vocation.

In 1987, due to its sale to Viscofan, the Cooperative Ian separated from the Group. This Cooperative had been the most significant in terms of turnover.

FORECAST HIGHLIGHTS FOR THE GROUP AS OF 31.12.1990

Sales:	4,386 Mptas.
Exports/sales:	3.60 %
Net profit:	75 Mptas.
Workforce:	294
% of profits set aside for returns which are pooled:	0

BERTAKO S. Coop., Areta Industrial Estate, Pamplona.

13) GOIKOA (1985)

(Cooperatives which make up the Group: Bertako, Embega, Gaiko, Oihana, Ortza, Sakana)

In 1980, in order to provide the eight Cooperatives associated with Caja Laboral and located in Navarra with common services, the Naeko Group was created.

In 1985, this group was divided for geographical reasons, with the five Cooperatives located in Pamplona and to the north of this city forming the Goikoa Group. The corresponding Organizational Regulations were approved and a common structure established, which has survived intact until today, except for the incorporation of a Social Director in 1987.

The departure of Ian and Zertan from Naeko meant that Embega joined Goikoa, as part of the GCM's general policy of extending and consolidating the Local Groups.

FORECAST HIGHLIGHTS FOR THE GROUP AS OF 31.12.1990	
Sales:	4,279 Mptas.
Exports/sales:	16.50 %
Net profit:	182 Mptas.
Workforce:	390
% of profits set aside for returns which are pooled:	20

14) MUGALDE (1986)

(Cooperatives which make up the Group: Biurrarena, Danona Litografía, Guria OP, Oiarso, Tajo)

As mentioned previously, in 1986, when Ikus XXI, Latz, Industrias Tajo and Litografía Danona applied to join the Orbide Group it was thought best to establish two Groups: Orbide and Mugalde. At present, each of these Groups consists of five Cooperatives.

When the previous Orbide Group was divided, its Central Services were also divided. In Mugalde these have maintained a significant structure which has not required important variations in the last two years, in spite of the big changes which have affected the Cooperatives which make up the Group.

FORECAST HIGHLIGHTS FOR THE GROUP AS OF 31.12.1990		
Sales:	9,646	Mptas.
Exports/sales:	1.60%	
Net profit:	93	Mptas.
Workforce:	626	
% of profits set aside for returns which are pooled:	0	

15) OTHERS

(Apart from the support bodies, there are four Cooperatives which have not been placed in any Local or sectorial Group: Alecop, Amat, Auzo-Lagun and Hertell).

The prospects for these Cooperatives as far as their integration in Groups is concerned are as follows:

-Amat should logically seek its place in the Fagor Group.

-Hertell should join the Goilan Group.

-Alecop and Auzo-Lagun, due to their peculiar structures, are the only Cooperatives in the GCM which are difficult to place in a Group. However, their incorporation in one of the nearby Local Groups must be seriously considered.

FORECAST HIGHLIGHTS FOR THE GROUP AS OF 31.12.1990	
Sales:	9,885 Mptas.
Exports/sales:	25.10 %
Net profit:	794 Mptas.
Workforce:	1,749
% of profits set aside for returns which are pooled:	0

c) The Mondragon Cooperative Group

After an uninterrupted period of thirty years in the creation of cooperatives and some twenty five years since the first Cooperative Group was formed, in 1982 and 1983 it was thought time to reflect on the need to create two "suprastructure bodies": **The Cooperative Congress and the General Council.**

It was stated as follows:

"Any form of updating ways of behaviour which may affect the organisation, should facilitate the consolidation of worker cooperativism and its development as a mitigating factor at least of the lack of entrepreneurialism evident and, consequently, acting decisively to create jobs. Anything which is inclined to strengthen the GROUP should be considered necessary and worth emphasising at times noted for their lack of initiative ... proceeding to the generation of employment and achieving subsequent well-being for the benefit of workers."

To conclude the following definitions were made:

*"1) **The Cooperative Congress,** which is given the capacity to maintain and develop the Cooperative Principles.*

*"2) **The Council of Groups** (now the General Council), given the capacity to manage the Group."*

It was thought time to crown the integration process of the Group: **Training of cooperators —> Cooperatives —> Cooperative Groups —> Mondragón Cooperative Group.**

Indeed, the **Basic Articles** of the Cooperative Congress and the General Council were drawn up, and then approved on 19th December 1984 *"with the character of a constitutional charter".*

It is worth taking note of the scope of the Cooperative Congress to achieve its objectives: *"to maintain, perfect and promote the essential aspects of our Cooperative Experience",* which cover:

a) Treatment of basic production factors (Work and Capital) in the Cooperatives of the Group.

b) Drawing up models for basic documents to control the operation of the Cooperatives (Statutes, Internal Regulations and Rules).

c) Drawing up basic policies dealing with fundamental aspects of common interest, such as:

- Sectorial grouping of the Cooperative Group

- Promotion of new Cooperatives

- Scientific and Technological Research

- Business and Cooperative Training

- Social Security for Cooperators

d) Creation of bodies in common ...

e) Definition of common directives

f) Analysis and definition of the function of the Cooperative Group

g) Development of external institutional relationships...

h) Analysis, debate and updating of the Cooperatives Principles on which the Experience is based".

Likewise, the Basic **Functions of the General Council** cover the following areas:

a) Policy on industry, research, investment, labour relations, finance, promotion and Social Security.

b) Coordination

c) Promotion

d) Arbitration

e) Control

f) Self-control and

g) Executive

Finally on 23rd September 1988 the **Permanent Commission of the General Council** approved document 0-88.1 "Attribution of Faculties and Organisation", which was limited to the following basic faculties:

a) Business Promotion

b) Cooperative Education

c) Institutional Relations

This step seems to have covered, dynamically and faithfully, the supposed reasons behind the experience over a third of a century, as a culmination of an entire process to shape the cooperative experience.

Inevitably all this incessant and tense development must be seen as conclusive proof of a work about to close an institutional cycle and which, however, has not exhausted its continually renewed vitality.

We find ourselves on the threshold of a change in direction of the Group, forced now to consider the development of new activities and, with these, to increase employment to generate well-being.

It would be stimulating, on reaching the roof of the institutional building, to observe that the parts which have served as its foundations have not forgotten their beginnings and the moral commitment with our Country through the rest: those who wish to work but cannot and whose mission concern us due to our original vocation.

5.4 CONSUMER COOPERATIVISM: **EROSKI**

The San José Consumer Cooperative began operating in Mondragón in 1958. It was one of the Cooperatives which created Caja Laboral Popular and the one which gave its premises for Caja Laboral's headquarters until 1974.

But it took more than ten years for the consumer cooperatives (supply and service of goods) associated with Caja Laboral Popular to be moulded into businesses because a different disposition, knowledge and management sensibility was required from those necessary in the mainly industrial producer cooperatives.

Once its Statutes were approved by the Ministry of Work on 11th August 1969 **Comerco** was born (changing its name to **Eroski** on 1st December 1970). This cooperative reconciles in the one institution worker-members, on the one hand, who work, carry out and manage and consumer-members, on the other, who were to be served specifically by the cooperative.

At that time, there were more than ten cooperatives in the form of shops in different towns in the Basque Country which had got together to create a model for service enterprises

to compare with those in the industrial sector which had achieved sufficient size, technical prestige and social recognition.

Eroski is a consumers' and users' cooperative whose combined result is comparable to the cooperative groups in its size, diversified activities and its origins. It was created through the merger of various consumer cooperatives, all associated with CLP, which were looking for greater business integration, to which end they managed to increase their size, centralise their services and achieve a consolidated company model, the immediate aims of which were to increase purchasing power, improve profitability and the inherent economies of scale.

Eroski today

* Sales

Turnover in 1990 will be approximately 78,000 million pesetas, an increase of 31% compared with the previous year.

Of this total 66,000 million pesetas corresponds to the sale of foodstuffs and the remaining 12,000 million to the non-food range (household goods, textiles, domestic appliances).

This level of sales reinforces its position as the leading retail company in the Basque Country. It occupies ninth position in the national ranking.

* Investment

The amount of investment carried out over 1990 will be close to 13,000 million pesetas.

As is now normal, most of this investment is for new shopping centres, with 8,700 million pesetas used for mainly medium and large size stores, with a sales area of more than 1,500 square metres.

* Workforce

The expansion of the cooperative is paralleled by an increase in the workforce. At the end of the year Eroski will have around 2,600 workers, which has meant the creation of 700 new jobs.

* The Eroski Commercial Network

As of 31.1.90, Eroski will have the following commercial outlets:
-4 "Hyper-Eroski"
-6 "Maxi-Eroski"

-78 "Super-Eroski"

-220 "Erosle" franchise outlets

-2 "Cash-Eroski"

-12 specialised textile and domestic appliance shops

- 16 "Eroski-Bidaiak" Travel Agency branches

Total sales area amounts to 117,000 square metres.

* Development

Eroski will continue with its expansion plan, reinforcing its leadership position, by means of the creation of all types of establishments, but extensively with the "hyper" and "maxi" models.

Likewise, in the rest of Spain, the "maxi" and "hyper" models shall be introduced with the collaboration of the Consum cooperative from Valencia.

Equally, an attempt will be made to tackle the French market, with the development of different models, and in collaboration with French regional cooperatives. This model shall be developed progressively in a necessary attempt to become a truly European company.

*uring the first fifteen years industrial cooperativism had technological support, mainly through technical assistance contracts signed with foreign companies from 1956*

5.5 RESEARCH

IKERLAN

During the first fifteen years industrial cooperativism had technological support, mainly through technical assistance contracts signed with foreign companies from 1956 onwards.

However it was necessary to overcome the dangerous technical subordination that this situation implied, because in a short time exports were to be the key to the extension of the well protected but more and more insufficient domestic market, and such licences were generally negotiated, with the express condition that no sales could be made abroad.

In 1968 thoughts first turned to this matter and took shape in the Eskola Politeknikoa, with the first steps in research taking place, due to a complete lack of material means, in the basements under the classroom buildings. During this period the pioneer cooperators underwent a certain austerity although, in turn, they had the hope that could surmount the barriers of ignorance, a certain degree of institutional inertia and their lack of total conviction.

In any case, the idea of tackling technical research themselves and achieving a certain degree of independence, was a serious goal for many cooperative managers, who finally took the necessary steps while using as their basis the report entitled *"Towards a Research Centre"*, drawn up in July 1973.

The moment was right and the initiative grouped together:

-Eskola Politeknikoa, which had created an R & D unit to study new technology.

-Caja Laboral Popular, committed to the creation of infrastructures which would consolidate the cooperative movement, and

-a group of cooperatives prepared to take on responsibility for the financing necessary to make the project a reality.

In order to define exactly what type of installations were required a programme of visits was prepared to fifteen or so national and foreign centres, with the aim of analyzing the methodology to be followed and to define a model of work. The initial process ended in March 1974 with a joint meeting which gave the green light to the initiative.

In its first phase the research team consisted of six people whose initial aim was to cut down the process between the appearance of technologies and their introduction in the academic world. When the project was taken on, the objective adopted was the *"mastery of technology for application in industry"*.

Whilst this experience received legal cover from Eskola, at the same time work had started on what would later be the permanent location of Ikerlan.

The fruit of this **second phase**, which then counted on twenty or so people, was the design and construction of the "Gizamat" industrial robots, pioneers in their day as they were the first designed with home-grown technology. In human terms the development of the centre was fast and the projects and technological diffusion plans followed one after the other in a dynamic fashion.

IKERLAN, Technological Research Centre

1982 produced a landmark in the history of Ikerlan, when it received recognition through official backing from the Basque Government. Five research centres configure and give support and technological cover to the programmes and activities emanating from the Basque Administration.

Today, the Ikerlan of the 90's, is an Ikerlan integrated in European research programmes. The centre has several years of experience in this new framework, and is conscious that service to the industrial sector must have a level of quality and technological depth comparable to the best centres in the European Community. As the final link in the process, Ikerlan has been admitted in EACRO, an organism which groups together the most select contract research centres in Europe.

The Ikerlan Philosophy

Ikerlan has always been defined as an Applied Research Centre, based on technology, which translated into practical terms means that knowledge is subordinated to the application - basically industrial - to which it is put. The technological activities of Ikerlan can be synthesised in the following trilogy:

. identification and selection,
. assimilation and generation,
. transfer and dissemination,

all with a specific objective in mind: "To transfer state-of-the-art technology to companies".

The working method is based on a balance between new technological knowledge and mastery - acquired through Research or Generic Projects - and the industrial applications carried out on demand - Industrial or Specific Projects-. The economic balance in the distribution of man/hours between one and the other type of project is a constant aim.

Financing

Financing depends on the type of the work. Research projects - those enabling the centre to advance in the mastering of technology - are financed by Basque Institutions while industrial projects on demand from companies finance the rest of the budget.

- millions of pesetas -

FINANCING	1985	1986	1987	1988	1989	1990
Research Projects	140.0	182.0	206.6	244.8	262.0	302.2
Projects and Services	134.8	153.1	228.3	290.8	299.5	365.9
Fees	30.1	37.5	36.8	38.6	44.7	54.5
Infrastructure aid	32.0	48.9	59.3	70.4	74.1	65.7
Others	6.0	11.4	8.2	11.5	15.2	15.0
TOTAL	342.9	432.9	539.2	656.1	695.5	803.3
INVESTMENT						130.0
• Own Funds						51.3
• Public Funds						78,7

Staff

This is one of the major concerns for all research institutions. As Ikerlan is a cooperative, most of its staff are worker-members.

STAFF	1985	1986	1987	1988	1989	1990
Permanent staff	58	67	67	65	72	77
Scholarship holders	10	13	13	19	16	20
EP(*) Teachers 1/2 day	5	4	5	3	3	3
Temporary contracts	3	2	6	13	15	21
1/2 day assistants	25	31	34	38	42	43
Foreign residents	-	-	-	-	-	5
TOTAL..........................	102	117	125	138	148	169

(*) Eskola Politeknikoa

The other two groups of people on which the Centre depends are:

-Engineering students from Eskola Politeknikoa who work in Ikerlan as half day assistants (Alecop). They represent an important source for future members.

-Scholarship holders and contracted staff who, having completed higher education, join Ikerlan for a period of 1-2 years to develop determined technologies. They are also a significant source for staff.

Technological Fields

Ikerlan's technology activities are carried out in three fields, which are technological activities in themselves and complementary, offering technology to the industrial sector.

Design and manufacturing technologies

   -CAD/CAM

   -Mechanical Engineering

   -Robotics and advanced automation

   -Design and management of production systems

Information technology

   -Automatics and control engineering

   -Artificial vision and sensorial systems

   -Processing and communications architecture

   -Artificial intelligence

Energy

   -Energy in buildings

   -Renewable energy

   -Energy in industry

Work carried out in 1990 (summary)

PROJECTS AND SERVICES

. Research Projects	8
. Industrial Projects	50
. International Projects	
. EEC (3 approved start of 1990)	5
. EUREKA	3
. Space (ESA)	1
. Studies and Services	40
. In collaboration with	51 companies

TECHNOLOGICAL DISSEMINATION (1989)

. Seminars and Courses	176 companies
	227 people
. Articles and Lectures	15
. Guidance for University Projects	9

IDEKO

In 1981, shortly after the creation of the Debako Group, this Group felt the need for a Research Centre, capable of meeting the technological requirements which, in a market as active and in constant evolution as that for machine tools, were practically impossible to satisfy at the individual company level.

Under these circumstances, taking advantage of the human and technological potential of the R & D units of the companies in the DEBAKO Group, a long training period for engineers was programmed, as a preliminary and essential step in the establishment of a specialised Research Centre within the Group. The idea was, by means of centralisation, to strengthen part of the R & D departments in the Group, with the capability to understand, assimilate, develop and transfer to companies, new techniques based on electronics, bearing in mind that, foreseeably, they were going to give rise to a new basic technological conception, as has in fact occurred.

With the mediation and help of Caja laboral Popular, after some preliminary experiences, IDEKO was created in 1986, as a machine tool R & D Centre, by the following cooperatives: Danobat, Goiti, Izarraitz, Lealde, Ona-Pres, Ortza, Soraluce, Txurtxil and the Ikerlan Research Centre.

From the start, the main aim of IDEKO was centred on collaboration with its members, in order to ensure that the products developed and manufactured were competitive in the international market. It was also born with the idea of helping to plan and coordinate a technological policy in the machine tool and advanced technology capital goods fields. About twenty researchers now work in this Centre, trying to understand and assimilate the complex world of new technology. They are divided into three departments: Mechanics, Electronics and Production Systems.

The design of structures, using the finite element method, technical support in CAD/CAM and the general design of machines are jobs normally carried out by the Mechanics Department. The Electronics Department carries out research in the field of numerical control, communications, artificial intelligence, sensorisation, etc., while the Production Systems Department develops software for simulating flexible manufacturing systems (FMS) in real time, and works on the integration of advanced manufacturing systems in DNC and in in-plant data acquisition.

By forming combined work teams with engineers from member companies, IDEKO has lead various highly complex technological projects amongst which it is worth mentioning the following: Soraluce flexible systems; flexible transfer installed in Ford to machine exhaust pipe families; high technology transfer which includes two robots, automatic measurements of parts, etc., supplied by Danobat and Soraluce to Zetor in Czechoslovakia, to machine gearbox casing families.

In 1990 work has been carried out on a gantry laser for cutting and welding with six controlled axes and mobile optics and in punching and bending flexible cell system with automatic loading and unloading and a blank store. Likewise, work has been carried out on a flexible cell, consisting of a lathe, machining centre, grinder and robot, manufactured by Danobat for Vocational Training.

At the start of 1988, after two years of experience and consolidation, having demonstrated that IDEKO was a valid and necessary project, the decision was taken to build a separate premises, to expand the research departments and to create a prototype workshop, in order to analyze and optimise the development process, checking, tests and validation of new products before their launch on the market.

In May 1990 the new IDEKO building was inaugurated, located on a 6,000 m^2 plot of land on the Arriaga Industrial Estate in Elgoibar. The building occupies 3,100 m^2, of which 1,500 m2 contain research rooms and laboratories and the remaining 1,500 m2 house the prototype workshop. The investments made since the creation of IDEKO, in computing equipment, buildings, installations, etc. exceed 400 million pesetas.

5.6 LAGUN-ARO IN THE FINANCIAL SYSTEM

In 1990 the financial reserves of Lagun-Aro exceeded 90,000 million pesetas. Their application to obtain the necessary profitability is determined by Law, its Statutes and the practice of prudence advised by the nature of such mutualist institutions in their operational and investment management.

In order to develop an activity of greater efficiency than pure intermediary investment, from the start of the 80's Lagun-Aro has undertaken to create financial entities through which it has generated cooperative employment within Lagun-Aro, Services Cooperative. It has also increased the value added produced by its reserves and managed to achieve greater overall profitability for its funds.

a) Aroleasing, S.A.

AROLEASING is a financial entity dedicated to leasing, with the aim of strengthening the production investment plans of small and medium sized companies, along with family businesses.

Lagun-Aro, Voluntary Social Welfare Entity, is the main shareholder and owner of Aro-Leasing.

The company, in its fourth year of activity, is well implanted in the Basque Country, and well known in the principal centres of the Spanish market. Moreover, because of its integration in the Mondragón Cooperative Group, it has signed collaboration agreements with the capital equipment manufacturing companies of the Group and with Caja Laboral Popular.

In 1989 Aroleasing grew substantially, with 14,340 million pesetas of new production and 19,040 million pesetas of exposure.

he initial drive behind the creation of the Company came from Lagun-Aro, Voluntary Social Welfare Fund, due to its links with and experience in social welfare. This led to the participation and involvement of Caja Laboral Popular on equal terms with Lagun-Aro."

Fixed assets earmarked for leasing net of deprerciations, went from 2,666 million pesetas in 1987 to 13,067 in 1989, and the future quotas for leasing went from 3,928 million pesetas in 1987 to 19,040 in 1989. Profit before transfers was 207 million pesetas, which was 2.08% over average live investment for the year.

The Company has adopted the criteria of strengthening its own resources to the maximum, so constituted share capital is 800 million pesetas, and reserves total 171 million. Moreover, the transfers for the provision of bad debts are at 1.5% over exposure, as a means of guaranteeing the solvency of the company.

As far as the management of liabilities is concerned, Aroleasing obtains its financing from the loans it receives from Lagun-Aro, Voluntary Social Welfare Fund, from lines of credit from finance companies and from the issue of company notes with an issue to the value of 3,500 million pesetas in 1989. In the future, the latter two sources of finance will be those used habitually.

Lastly, as a result of the fact that leasing companies depend on the Bank of Spain, since the new law regulating Credit Institutions, an inspection was carried out of Aroleasing by the Bank of Spain, in which correct compliance with all requirements established by law for leasing companies was verified.

Head Offices of Seguros Lagun-Aro in Aretxabaleta, Guipúzcoa

b) Seguros Lagun-Aro, S.A.

When SEGUROS LAGUN-ARO (an insurance company) was created in 1982, it came into being with close links to the Cooperative Group, in an attempt to channel the demand for insurance in that sphere, providing advice on the subject of insurance for the cooperatives and recovering part of the costs necessary for the protection of the material assets of the Group. At the same time, it was proposed that the offer of financial services should be extended outside the Group, through insurance, with the resulting transfer of external funds.

The initial drive behind the creation of the Company came from Lagun-Aro, Voluntary Social Welfare Fund, due to its links with and experience in social welfare. This led to the participation and involvement of Caja Laboral Popular on equal terms with Lagun-Aro, due to the nature of the project, which was in the general interest of the Group. At that time, it was decided to create a limited company, for economic-financial reasons, given that the urgent need for capital excluded the cooperative formula, characteristic of our Group.

In its first phase the Company specialised in industrial products, aimed at average sized cooperatives. During this period, the role of reinsurance was fundamental, as without it the development of Seguros Lagun-Aro would have been slower.

In 1983 turnover was 39 million pesetas, rising, in 1984, to 108, of which 55% corresponded to industrial policies.

In its second phase, whose start coincided with the appearance of the Private Insurance Regulations (Reglamento de Ordenación del Seguro Privado), Seguros Lagun-Aro started to open up to the market outside the cooperatives, looking especially to household economies. This created a need to increase the number of sales outlets, which were covered by employees of the company itself, contrary to the criteria prevailing in the sector.

By the end of 1986 the volume of premiums issued ha risen to 493 million pesetas, with equity exposure havingreduced its participative weight to 31.5%.

Throughout 1987, 1988 and 1989 new alternative forms were sought to channel the network, to which end commercial collaboration was established with Caja Laboral Popular's network of branches. Since 1989, through the Insurance Brokers, Caja Laboral Popular offers legal cover to the insurance intermediation activity.. Likewise, as part of this policy, it also collaborates with Aroleasing.

In July 1989, the Italian company Unipol bought its way into the share capital of Seguros Lagun-Aro, taking up 30% of the capital, which was increased to 586 million pesetas.

The increase in turnover in 1989 was higher than the average for the sector, with the volume of premiums issued totalling 2,662.5 million pesetas. Of this volume, 71.8% corresponded to car insurances which, however, grew less than in the rest of the sector, demonstrating the need to purge the portfolio initiated that year, in order to reestablish the technical equilibrium.

As far as the future is concerned, in 1990 the Strategic Plan was drawn up to define the direction the Company will take for the three year period 1990/1992. There is an agreement to increase the number of shareholders in the Company, by means of incorporating various European insurance companies with links to the social economy, which should strengthen Seguros Lagun-Aro's position in the European transnational market.

Moreover, Seguros Lagun-Aro will continue to concentrate its efforts on significantly increasing its market share in the Basque Country, at the same time as initiating a strategy for progressive expansion in the rest of Spain.

The increase in market share shall be carried out in such a way as to reduce the participative weight of car insurance in the product portfolio, by means of establishing a commercial collaboration plan with agents and insurance brokers, intensifying, in turn, collaboration with Caja Laboral Popular and other financial institutions.

 *EGUROS LAGUN-ARO VIDA, S.A. was created in July 1988, with a share capital of 320 million pesetas."*

c) Seguros Lagun-Aro Vida, S.A.

When Seguros Lagun-Aro, S.A. was created, the decision not to operate in life insurance was justified by the basic consideration that, given the small size of the market and the effort that would be required to achieve a sufficient share in that market, this question should not be tackled until Seguros Lagun-Aro, S.A. had consolidated its structure.

Since then, things have changed somewhat. Seguros Lagun-Aro, S.A. has achieved a modest share of the market in general insurance and is undergoing a period of expansion. On the other hand, the formerly small life insurance market is increasing in size considerably, and not only due to the effect of the "single premiums".

These circumstances led to the decision, in 1988, that the moment was right to extend the company's activities into life insurance. Therefore, in July 1988, SEGUROS LAGUN-ARO VIDA, S.A. was created, with a share capital of 320 million pesetas.

Subsequently, the Government, taking advantage of the authorization given by a law passed in 1984, undertook a revaluation of capital, raising the minimum required to operate in life insurance from 320 million pesetas to 1,500 million, in an attempt to eliminate a marginal offer in this market, with little guarantee of continuity in the long term.

In July 1989, Compagnia Assicratrice Unipol, S.p.A, joined the shareholders of the Company, with a majority holding, with 70% of share capital. The remaining 30% is held in equal shares by Caja Laboral popular and Lagun-Aro, Voluntary Social Welfare Fund.

At the same time, the Company increased its share capital to the minimum legally established limits, that is to say, 1,500 million pesetas. On 26th December 1989, the company received authorization from the Directorate General for Insurance to operate in life insurance.

Moreover, the first steps have been taken to clarify and set the limits for the commercial model, and the projection of a national commercial network, an expansion which has been identified as the key, in competitive terms, on which, to a great extent, the future success of the Company depends.

GENERAL ORGANISATIONAL CHART OF THE MONDRAGON COOPERATIVE GROUP (SECTORIAL)

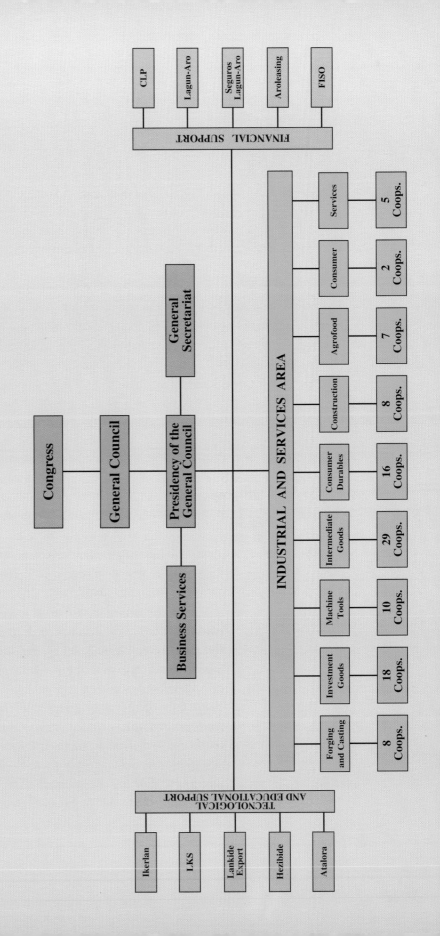

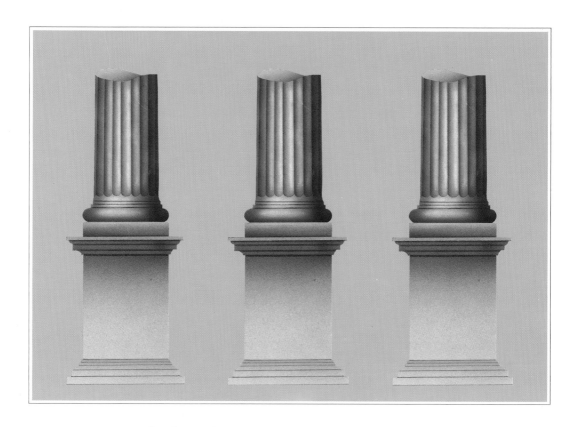

"The cooperative worker "*does not have to be a deserter from the glorious world of the workers, who today are not fortunate enough to work in the same conditions of economic and social emancipation*", he cannot look or act like a member of the "*nouveau riche*", or of the labour aristocracy. "*It would be a poor concept for the world to have of a cooperativism which served for nothing more than creating other minorities with a higher level of wellbeing. That is to say, minorities to be simply added to those we already have in the bourgeois world. So responsibility should lead us to feel solidarity with other workers. For us responsibility and solidarity are inseparable*". (J. Mª Arizmendiarrieta)*

6. THE BASIC PRINCIPLES OF THE MONDRAGON COOPERATIVE EXPERIENCE

The establishment of a code of conduct which would formally gather together the aspirations of the pioneers of the Experience - especially those voiced by Don José María Arizmendiarrieta -, and the daily message (the practical accumulation of which already constitutes an institutional legacy), were developed and approved by the 1st Mondragón Cooperative Group Congress held on 2nd and 3rd October 1987.

Under the title "Basic Principles of the Mondragón Cooperative Experience" ten statements were drawn up giving shape and form to the ideas which we had been putting into practice over more than thirty years in the cooperatives of the Group.

Inevitably the Basic Principles have their roots and their definition - to a large extent - in the fundamentals of the International Cooperative Alliance. The operational framework is based on the legislation controlling cooperativism, in its different classes. But in their practical definition and in their scope they go beyond the strict limits established by concepts or by regulations, with the emergence of criteria like those expressed in 6) Payment Solidarity and 8) Social Transformation especially, which contain elements of our own, embodied in a specific time and a specific country, which the Mondragon Cooperative Experience has tried to satisfy and serve.

The method we are going to follow consists of systematically comparing each principle with the text which is used in practice, either in the Statutes or Regulations of the various institutions of the Group and in a more recent document laying down the Bases of the Congress.

It will also be useful to include some of the singular writings of the unceasing teaching of Don José María Arizmendiarrieta, whose place in the analysis of each "Principle" represents, in addition to its aesthetic value through the timeliness and adornment of his ideas, an ethical complement with a notably pedagogical hallmark.

By way of an introduction, the exhortation which follows is a global way of interpreting, in their essential aspects, the motives which inspired the experience:

"This Experience corresponds to a new spirit of confidence in man and his capabilities. In this case it revives the sense of freedom, dignity and justice, undeniably woven into the traditional and democratic institutions of our land and, therefore, exponents of the idiosyncrasy of its people.

One of our characteristics has been our practical sense, knowing how to act within the scope of our possibilities, without indifference or without abandoning our ideals. We have known how to take hold of and not to waste opportunities for the common good. Processes of association are not viable without moderation, with consent from all sides normally meaning that everyone has to give way a little from their respective positions. Radical positions go against the most steadfast qualities of our country and the human and social virtues of its people.

This we declare and desire, exemplifying the spirit of a people more inclined to action rather than speculation, to being rather than to having, to progress rather than to domination, fond and jealous of their liberty and their privileges, of the environment necessary for multi-faceted self-realisation in work and, through work, for the common good". (José María Arizmendiarrieta) (J.M.A.)

1. OPEN ADMISSION

The Mondragón Cooperative Experience declares itself open to all men and women who accept these Basic Principles and prove themselves professionally capable of carrying out the jobs available.

Therefore, to join the *Experience*, there shall be no discrimination on religious, political, and ethical grounds, nor due to gender. The only requirement shall be respect for its internal constitution.

Open admission is the main guiding principle in the activities and relations between people in cooperative development.

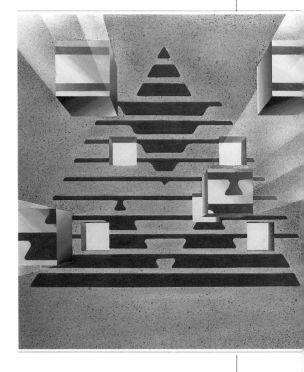

The legal framework which upholds this principle is very extensive in the different Institutions of the Group, and it is evident not only through the positive possibilities it offers, but even more so through the permanent progress in the creation of employment, achieved thanks to the restrained distribution of profits mainly destined for non-distributable reserves with the clear aim of promoting incessant activity and facilitating open admission for new members.

In the current statutes of the worker cooperatives the desire for openness is formulated as follows ...*"any one capable of working and carrying out their work in the Cooperatives can become worker-members, provided that, conscious of the rights and obligations assumed when subscribing to these Statutes, they undertake to discharge them with loyalty and efficiency"*.

"T*he main form of basic justice is that which we should practice with each other, considering ourselves to be free men and women"* (J.M.A.)

Moreover, sensitive to the socioeconomic situation in the Basque Country, a turbulent region in political terms, guarantees are amply provided by adding that ...*"the political, union or religious beliefs, or race, language, gender or marital status of the applicant, unless incompatible with the authorised activities of the cooperative, shall not be cause for refusing admission"*.

Limitations are only established on the basis of practical needs as they are defined by the number of worker- members required to manage, administer and make the cooperative work and by the reports drawn up at the end of the trial period, strictly subject to current legislation.

As far as joining Caja Laboral Popular is concerned, the same selection criteria is followed.

With regard to collective members - legal entities -, the criteria, previously established by law, and now internally by the statutes, is that only the following can be members: *"cooperatives, as well as other entities in which Caja Laboral Popular has an equity interest, or its associated cooperatives ... the members of the cooperatives associated with Caja Laboral Popular"* and the staff of this Credit Institution.

This is how the Caja functions as a first degree cooperative in which primacy, expressed in the General Assemblies, is exercised subsequently by each individual member, with their own vote, and the cooperatives, in relation to the number of members they have.

Open admission is thus perfectly safeguarded in the light of the principles which inspired cooperativism, but obviously limited by the technical requirements of the cooperative as an enterprise.

As far as these limitations are concerned, the situations are quite different.

With respect to **consumer cooperatives**, there are practically no limitations at all: the greater the number of members the greater the potential sales capacity, and for this reason the associative barriers are fixed at a minimum with the capital contribution reduced to a symbolic figure, in the form of a joining fee, in strict compliance with the Law. Thus, Eroski, the only consumer cooperative in the Group, has lifted the associative barriers on the understanding that, technically speaking, a certain critical mass of sales is necessary to guarantee stable profitability, and an extensive number of members to maintain, within the framework of this profitability, the company's unmistakable condition as a consumer cooperative.

The same is not true of **worker cooperatives**. In their case, open admission, as a right of any citizen, depends on the technical necessity of the cooperative based on productivity (quantity) and the singularity of its organisation (quality).

As regards **quantity**, it is immediately obvious that it is impossible to make an unlimited increase in the number of worker-members compatible with productivity and profitability, guided, in the market place, by the search for a strict reduction of costs, a variable for which the payment of labour is a decisive component.

And **quality** establishes a clear selection, not included in positive norms, based on the compatibility of the post to be covered with the candidates for that post. In simple terms, the cooperative, on complying with the personal concepts of a generic nature expressed in its Statutes, must choose those candidates who show themselves to be most capable of carrying out the jobs vacant in the organisation or which are created.

Open admission in the Group's Credit Cooperative - Caja Laboral Popular - is limited to four key conditions:

-Association with legal entities.

-That they be cooperatives or entities in which the associates and CLP itself participate significantly.

-That CLP maintains sufficient capacity to finance new members, without the risk of a concentration of credit.

-That in the objective examination of the technical reports, nothing is found to oppose admission.

Under the different models of behaviour, backed by technical evaluations which tend towards the efficient promotion of the cooperative, open admission takes on a key role in the model of conduct which the Group has adopted throughout its history.

2. DEMOCRATIC ORGANISATION

The *Mondragón Cooperative Experience* proclaims the basic equality of its worker-members with respect to their rights to be, to possess and to know, which implies the acceptance of a democratic organisation of the company, specified in:

a) The primacy of the General Assembly, made up of all the members, and which operates on the principle of "one member, one vote".

b) The democratic organisation of the governing bodies, specifically the Governing Council, which is responsible to the General Assembly in respect of to its management.

c) The collaboration with the management bodies designated to manage the company by delegation of the entire community. These bodies shall have sufficient authority to carry out their functions efficiently for the common good.

Democratic organisation is developed in the way it is accessible in a company in which the dynamism necessary to optimise management should prevail, leaving the decisions to be taken by the administrators ..."once the most suitable have been chosen to govern the cooperative".

The participation of the membership is established by means of operating in a situation of equality, giving one vote to each member of the worker cooperatives, for their participation in decision making in the General Assembly; neither the capital contribution nor the post occupied, nor the seniority or hours worked are taken into account.

"The General Assembly, made up of the members, is the supreme body for *the expression of the will of the membership".*

"**D**emocracy, once adopted in a noble fashion, automatically leads to discipline, responsibility, to the consolidation of solidarity, in short, to authentic social progress". (J.M.A.)

144

Through these regulations which constitute the systematic application of the cooperative principles and by means of the laws which back them up, the field of participation is widened when amongst the inalienable rights of the members the following stand out:

- To elect and be elected to form part of the bodies of the cooperative, as well as to elect, and be elected representatives of the same in the institutions of which the cooperative forms part.

- To participate, with the right to speak and vote, in the adoption of agreements made by the General Assembly and by the other internal bodies of which they form part.

- To be informed about any matter related to the cooperative.

By way of the right to information and participation, a model of democracy is defended which permits and favours a process of self-management on the part of the workers, members of the cooperative, who have an authentic role to play in community terms in basic management.

Thus, in the General Assembly the right is given to "approve general policies and strategy" and the financial and economic system which may affect the social and equity development of the cooperative.

However, and in spite of the recognition of these rights and their reiterated proclamation, this does not necessarily lead to the permanent exercising of full democracy insofar as there is extensive delegation of power. The level of knowledge - the key for taking lucid decisions - is very different from one member to another, and, in any case, the method of direct consultation cannot be repeated assiduously, or so repeatedly as to satisfy the desires of each and every member.

Democratic organisation therefore boils down, to a great extent, to the election of the Governing Council, elected for four years, with half of its members to be replaced every two years, and to the appointment, through this Governing Council, of the complete executive team, in whom, in fact - rarely has a presidentialist cooperative arisen - the economic, social and strategic fortunes of the company are delegated.

It is therefore extremely important that the members of the Governing Council be elected prudently so that after democracy has been exercised the objectives pursued are achieved: to attain the optimum development of the cooperatives within the framework of equal rights to possess - by means of the fair distribution of the wealth generated - and to know, through systematic, truthful and sufficient information, within the reach of each member, the most detailed development of the principal social and economic factors of the cooperative.

In this way the democratic organisation of the cooperatives has, due to its essential nature, traits of its own which can guide it, unequivocally, via the indirect mandate of majority agreements.

It must be admitted that, in spite of everything, as happens in all institutions, not all mem bers have the same level of involvement to really get inside the problems concerning the cooperative, and nor are all members inclined to exercise the rights they have with the same level of intensity.

The inalienable principle, on the basis of which each member has a vote to be used freely, can thus be channelled, as a legitimate use of democratic assumptions, in favour of certain currents, the risk of which would not, in any case, be in the exercising of the democratic will, but in that the business function inscribed in any economic organisation, in the market economy, be distorted, and that the specific aims of the cooperative were supplanted by democratic means.

So the transparency in information, the equality of everyone as members and the method for calculating the social will used in the General Assemblies of the cooperatives constitute an organizational model which can only be compared to organizations of a different nature, be they political, associative, sporting or non-profit making organisations in which decisions are not taken in terms of the economic risk which each member holds, but giving each vote the personal value conferred by simply being a worker.

At the start of the experience the vote was qualified, weighted by the wage grade which, supposedly, measured precisely the amount of service each member gave the cooperative; this was also the basis for each member's economic remuneration. According to this criteria some members voted in accordance with the minimum grade and others with the maximum, which was limited to grade three.

This system was not popular, it was difficult to explain, it created discontent and, after all, in no way changed the results that would have been obtained if all members had exercised their right with just one vote each, in accordance with the basic principles of cooperativism.

For this reason the method was abolished about ten years after its introduction, eradicating an attempt to weight the right to participate in decision-making on the basis of knowledge of business or economic management.

In the Group, guided by the refined principle that those who work have a right to take part in the decisions made affecting their company, the institution of the worker-member has been generalised in cooperatives which are not worker cooperatives: Consumer and User Cooperatives, Credit Cooperatives and Service Cooperatives (Eroski, Caja Laboral Popular, Educational Cooperatives, Research Cooperatives, etc.).

In worker cooperatives men and women become members by contributing their own labour; in the other types of cooperatives mentioned, by definition, members and users, those who need financing or who cooperativise education or research and development services, become members.

In these cooperatives labour would have had to be hired, financed by the cooperative itself and these workers would not have had any right to a share in the profits nor to exercise democracy. This is what happens in consumer and credit cooperatives all over the world.

By extending the social and economic benefits of the cooperatives which are not worker cooperatives to their workers too - recognised at the request of the Mondragón Cooperative Group in the General Law on Cooperatives as worker-members, because they contribute their labour - four classes of cooperatives were created with two classes of members:

- Consumers and Users + Worker-members

- Credit Members + Worker-members

- Educational Service Members + Worker-members

- Research and Development Service Members + Worker-members

To perfect democratic organisation, always a delicate task, it is most important that all members have the same general interest in their cooperative and it is, or could at least be contradictory, for these interests and objectives to be opposed or not strictly coincidental.

The balance has been sought in Eroski by constituting a General Assembly in which there are consumer members and worker-members with equal representation; in Caja Laboral Popular the members who benefit from credit are predominant, as they were the cooperatives which created the institution. This membership duality has been resolved in service cooperatives, also known as mixed cooperatives, in the same terms. Their presence has made a balanced exercising of power difficult, but the effort made to cooperativise and democratise all the situations possible is evident.

In the end, it is a matter of ensuring that all the agents which provide a service are trustees of social primacy on which, in spite of certain inevitable restrictions, the essence of democracy rests.

It has to be agreed that it can never be known in an organisation if democracy prospers in all interstices of the decision making mechanisms and, more specifically, in Cooperatives in general and in those of the Group; but what is totally beyond doubt is that the cooperative system has such a high level of democracy that any fickleness in the management and the reiteration of errors, have in that democracy an irreplaceable mechanism for correction.

It is another thing whether it is used well. For this it is necessary to understand and apply with good sense the dictates of reason, directed towards solidary prosperity in the cooperative.

3. SOVEREIGNTY OF LABOUR

The *Mondragón Cooperative Experience* **considers that Labour is the principal factor for transforming nature, society and human beings themselves and, therefore:**

a) **Renounces the systematic contracting of salaried workers.**

b) **Gives Labour total primacy in the organisation of cooperatives.**

c) **Considers Labour to be worthy, in essence, in the distribution of the wealth created.**

d) **Manifests its will to extend the options for work to all members of society.**

The origins of the Mondragon Cooperative Group and the social atmosphere prevailing during the period of its consolidation in the Basque Country, meant that labour was pre-eminently extolled as the "principal factor for transforming nature ..." and fundamentally worthy of the wealth generated.

On this basis, it should be no surprise that thirty years later the criteria which in the 50's stimulated the Group's launch still hold firm. In practical terms this principle materialised with the establishment of the following as the most important norms: the renunciation of contracting salaried workers; the constitution of the General Assembly with the sum total of all worker-members; the distribution of income produced in terms of the work contributed, and the determined will of the Group to promote the creation of employment by extending the new company model.

"Man transforms and makes nature fertile through his work, and work is the greatest asset a community possesses". (J.M.A.)

The first chapter of this work explained some of the reasons behind the development of the Experience, based mainly on the practical difficulty of achieving, through traditional companies, the change necessary to give the worker a specific role in taking decisions which affected his own activity and his way of life.

The differences noted, from an analysis of the causes behind the launch of the Experience, between other thinkers and pioneers of Cooperativism are evident.

Don José María Arizmendiarrieta said that *"work is, primarily, a service to the community and a form of personal development"*, and he added *"... our people are conscious that their level of wellbeing and their strength have come from the potential for work of their offspring. These working reserves and contingents have been the armies with which we have promoted our historic personality and ... we are known throughout the world"*.

For his part George Jacob Holyoake, in his History of the Pioneers of Rochdale reminds us that the Rochdale Society of Equitable Pioneers *"...has as its aim and objective to obtain a pecuniary benefit and to improve the domestic and social conditions of its members, by means of saving a capital sum in order to put the following plans into practice:*

"To open a store to sell provisions, clothes, etc."

"To purchase or build a certain number of houses for its members"

"To initiate the manufacture of articles to provide work for members who were unemployed".

In Rochdale the principle of sharing profits with the consumers was established - customers *"without whom profits would not be possible"*.

The cooperativisation of work was started between 1854 and 1855, *"organising it in accordance with the principle of profit sharing for workers"*. However, in 1864, ten years later, the conclusion was that "the system of allowing the workers a share in the distribution of profits has been abandoned after having experimented with it".

In France, Charles Gide (28th June 1847 to 12th March 1932) was given *"a place apart in cooperativism, surrounded by the affectionate deference of all and sundry; and for those closest to him, due to his political convictions, he was the "master""*.

However, in his Programme in the Nîmes School, in a conference given in 1889 with the title Cooperation as an Economic Programme, he said concisely:

The **cooperativist programme** consists of three stages:

1. **Commercial Stage**

   Grouping of consumer cooperatives in order to, with their profits, set up large wholesale stores and make purchases on a large scale.

2. **Manufacturing Stage**

   With the capital created, start producing everything necessary for the needs of associated consumers: bread, flour, textiles and clothing, shoes, hats, soap, biscuits and paper.

3. **Agricultural Stage**

   Leave for the distant future the purchase of land and estates for the direct production of wheat, wine, oil, meat, milk, fat, eggs, fowls, vegetables, fruit, flowers and wood, which constitute the basis of consumption.

His speech went on to say: *"I am only too aware that it will probably seem utopian and irrelevant the idea that some consumer cooperatives can overcome step by step all the production forces of a country ...and thus it should be a reality that these consumer associations include not only the working classes, but the whole nation, also embracing, therefore, the moneyed classes".*

As for worker production associations, he did not hold out any great hope, saying: *"Most of these associations, in spite of the heroic efforts that must have been necessary to raise the world, have failed; and what is an even more serious symptom still ... they have sacrificed the principle which constitutes the soul of production cooperatives ., that is to say, the progressive emancipation of the working class".*

It is clear that Don José María Arizmendiarrieta continued firm in his convictions when he added: *"Man transforms and makes nature fertile through his labour, and labour is the greatest asset that the community possesses"*, and he concluded emphatically: *"to live with dignity, one must embrace work".*

Under these auspices which contain key concepts for understanding different mentalities, it can be seen that the cooperativism which was the forerunner to that developed by the *Mondragón Experience* was fundamentally consumer cooperativism, perhaps agricultural and, in a complementary way, credit cooperativism, in France, Germany and Italy.

Worker cooperativism was developed later in Italy and it is that of Mondragon which, under the emblematic declaration of a *"change in structure"*, raises the concept of the sovereignty of labour, establishing the company as the basic unit in the market economy.

The legal framework has been faithfully drawn up, giving practical form to the original hypothesis when it states that: *"any one capable of working and carrying out their work in the*

Cooperatives can become worker-members, provided that, conscious of the rights and obligations assumed when subscribing to these Statutes, they undertake to work loyally and efficiently".

As far as sharing the wealth generated is concerned, it was established that profits would be distributed amongst the members in proportion to the work carried out, measured by the amount received in terms of advance payments (wages in the case of employed workers) over the year. The notion, moreover, which aims to be clear, is completed by saying: *"in no case can profits be shared on the basis of participation in social capital".*

This insistence arose and led to the practice adopted in the early years of the cooperatives, in which, when it came to calculating the merits which were worthy of the profits of the cooperative, both interest on capital (6% net), on the one hand, and advance payments, on the other, were paid. On the basis of the sum of these two concepts, each member having their own total, the part of the profits to be shared out was distributed. Now profits are not distributed on the basis of the interest advanced on capital which, back then, was understood to represent the **effort of previous labour transformed into capital.**

The **"manifest will to extend options for work to all members of society"** was objectively developed and applied in the same distribution of profits defined in article 4, Distribution of Profits, of the Basic Regulations on the **Treatment of Social Capital**. These regulations make it compulsory to assign at least 50%, double the legally established percentage, to the non-distributable reserve fund or to the welfare fund, on the understanding that this socialises profits, strengthens the company technologically and accumulates the financial means to enable the development of new activities and jobs.

The *"renunciation of the systematic contracting of salaried workers"* is an aspiration which has passes through several stages.

During the first 24 years this principle was firmly and successf ully respected, and several cooperatives were unable to join Caja Laboral Popular - the financial axis of the *Experience* and forerunner of the corporative project, which was envisaged from the start - because to cover certain posts they contracted salaried workers. In short, this principle was a *"sine qua non"* for joining the group.

Subsequently, when unemployment rose in the Basque Country to 23% of the active population and the Government established incentives for the definitive placement of workers as members, the attitude changed and the cooperatives, in accordance with the Law, also contracted salaried workers.

In the face of this situation, which clearly disregards the principles solemnly approved in the 1st MCG Congress, there are two attitudes amongst the workers affected:

- That in which they know that, in all probability, they are going to be admitted as members and want to work as salaried workers so that at the end of this temporary period they can receive an unemployment compensation and then become definitive members, and pay their capital stake in the cooperative, and

- That of those admitted on a temporary basis, to cover temporary or seasonal vacancies who, aware of the fragility of their employment, prefer to become members immediately to guarantee their stable and/or definitive placement.

This is how a principle is being disregarded under the protection of an anomalous situation in which the permissiveness of the Government, the duplicity of individualism, a social climate which vindicates short term solutions, together with the managers' fear in the face of the threat of a drop in demand, (in a market economy as an expression of *"war by other means"* ever more surrounded by difficulties), all cast their shadows over a principle which was basic to the Group and the reason for its launch and subsequently, one of the symbols which most ennobled the social conduct of the Group.

Because in the *Experience*, compliance with written regulations was never the only guide, but the most demanding, being based on the ethical behaviour on which practical cooperativism should be built.

4. THE INSTRUMENTAL AND SUBORDINATE CHARACTER OF CAPITAL

The *Mondragón Cooperative Experience* considers Capital to be an instrument, subordinate to Labour, necessary for business development, and worthy, therefore, of:

a) **Remuneration, which is:**

- **Just, in relation to the efforts implied in accumulating capital.**

- **Adequate, to enable necessary resources to be provided.**

- **Limited in its amount, by means of corresponding controls.**

- **Not directly linked to the Profits made.**

b) **Availability subordinate to the continuity and development of the cooperative, without preventing the correct application of the principle of open admission.**

From the start, the need for capital to develop the Cooperative *Experience* has never been scorned or ignored by the Group. However, it was understood that where there were ideas, and enthusiasm to put them into practice, there would never be a lack of financial resources.

And that is what happened when the first cooperative was started up by 110 founder members who put up 20 million pesetas (some 300 million pesetas, once corrected to 1990 levels using the annual cost of living figures), for 16 members to start work in 1956 in Mondragón. At that time there was such a thing as an associate member: a member who contributed capital, subject to the cooperative regulations in relation to primacy and to the dividends paid on contributions.

*ooperativism without the structural capacity to attract and assimilate capital at the level of the requirements of industrial productivity is but a temporary solution, an invalid formula."*
(J.M.A.)

The ease with which profits were made meant that capital lost importance in the minds of the members, compared to the role of labour.

Therefore, to a certain extent, this basic principle expresses concepts which are reciprocal to those dealt with previously in the chapter on **sovereignty of labour**.

What is certain is that over a third of a century the attitude to dividends paid on capital has changed quite noticeably, although not in conceptual terms.

At the start, dividends consisted of four elements, each with characteristics of their own and, together, these four summarised the concept of just or equitable remuneration.

- **The first** element, or "basic income", applied was 4.5%, a dividend considered normal at the start of the *experience* when the inflation rate was around 5% (except in 1964 when it was 12.7%).

- **The second** element was called the "risk premium" and was set at 1.5%. It was only paid in those years when there were profits and it was applied *"in compensation for the risk that investment entailed"*; for this reason, once the value of the capital stake had been returned, by means of the repayment of this "risk premium" - 66 years would have been required - the right to receive it would come to an end.

- **The third** element arose from the criteria for the application of the cooperative returns, according to which the interest which resulted from adding "basic income" to the "risk premium", a figure of 6%, was added to the payment for work and formed part of the total amount worthy of the cooperative returns from the profits, or surplus, once taxes, transfers to the social welfare and reserve funds, had been deducted. These returns have been the equivalent of as much as 80% of advance payments, although more recently 20%, meaning that 1.2% was added to the 6% from the two previous elements: "basic income" (4.5%) + "risk premium" (1.5%) = 6%.

- **The fourth** element tried to correct monetary erosion, the product of inflation. Prior to this, fixed assets were regularised and, on the basis of the result obtained, the contributions were updated on 1st January each year.

Overall, the average dividends paid on capital over the first 20 years were around 13%, even though there were years when inflation exceeded 12% (1973 to 1983), in which, on occasion, dividends went above 20%, if one takes into account that the Consumer Price Index (CPI) was 26.4% in 1977.

During these years, in which the profits of the cooperatives fell, reflections were made on capital dividends.

From another more general perspective of control, a Law passed on 19th December 1974 established that interest paid on members' contributions could not exceed the basic rate set by the Bank of Spain plus three points, a criteria which was included in the Regulations in 1978 and then the Law which came into force on 2nd April 1987, which in effect limited the maximum interest which could be paid on capital to 11% annually.

It was never really clear whether other dividends could be added to this limit on the basis of the reserves created from the regularisation of the balance sheets, from time to time, authorised by the Spanish Treasury. In the Law of 1974 it was made specific that it would be applied *"under the same conditions and with the same benefits as established for ordinary companies"*.

The confluence of these limitations: little profit, high inflation and legal limitations, introduced new concepts which, however, included in part the original model of conduct.

Therefore Article 6: Determination of the Interest Rate to be paid on Capital, of October 1987, established the following as fair remuneration:

a) A maximum base gross interest rate of 7.5% annually.

b) An "inflation correcting" interest which as a maximum could be 70% of the increase in CPI for the previous year.

c) A maximum limit, between both elements, which should not exceed the legal limits, fixed for several years now at 11% (Bank of Spain base rate of 8% + 3 percentage points).

Element b) is applied when possible, because the Law so authorises, to the debit of the reserves created by the regularisation of the balance sheets although, by means of appropriate retentions, that is to say at greater cost, it can also be done to the debit of the profits of the cooperatives.

In this way, in the last few years the value of fixed assets has not been updated annually, because it is not authorised by Law, and interest on capital has been limited, at best, to a gross rate of 11%. However, net dividends, the only surplus which can be monetarised, have remained at 5.62%, although the intention was that they should be 6%, because as the retention on capital income was recently raised from 20% to 25%, 7.5% is now not sufficient to provide a net rate of 6%.

It will never be demonstrated that "fair remuneration" is achieved with an 11% rate of interest. With respect to inflation, now more under control at around 6% since 1987, the dividends are positive, but compared with the interest rates paid on fixed interest securities and even on time deposits, there is no stimulation to keep deposits in the Cooperatives of the Group.

This is why the connotation of "adequate remuneration" to encourage increases in capital and to obtain necessary resources, is a formula hardly used in other than cases of extreme need. But it is compulsory when, in the cooperative, equity has disappeared, and it is necessary to rebalance the balance sheet, with the cooperation of the Group and Caja Laboral Popular, because in that moment the increase to be made in capital by the members themselves is a prior condition to receiving subsequent financial support from the institutions of the Group.

The **limitations** in remuneration have therefore been clearly established and the sovereignty of labour consolidated as the generator of wealth.

As far as the independence of remuneration in relation to the profits of the cooperative is concerned, the criteria followed takes into account outside factors: the base rate of the Bank of Spain and inflation. In no case can profits modify this criteria, unless the cooperative is technically bankrupt or cash flow obtained is negative, in which case not even the fixed interest paid on capital is due.

With this set of criteria it is difficult to comply with the proposal for maintaining sufficient **availability** of social capital, especially in those cases in which members leave the cooperative or retire. The latter case is almost always when the member's capital stake is at its highest level. When members cease to be workers in the cooperative their capital stakes are returned and the equity of the cooperative is reduced, and so, therefore, is its solvency.

In reality it must be said that in the Cooperatives of the Group and, in general, in strictly applied cooperativism, there is no economic advantage in making capital contributions nor, if possible, in leaving rights acquired through labour in the cooperative, because the subordination intended means that no social rights are acquired. The limited remuneration is, in practice, a negative discrimination which in no way encourages contributions unless they are absolutely compulsory.

The creation of Caja Laboral Popular as the Group's financial institution was to cover the inevitable need for borrowing that any company has. Its cooperative nature and the fact that it was created by cooperatives, defined the scope of its support, little to do with exercising dominion and employing a policy of potential abuse in the application of interest and in the cost of the services rendered.

Thanks to this financing, which, in reality comes from the savings of the community, the cooperativism of Mondragón has been possible, and the future of the instrumental character of capital which has been sought, lies in the framework of real achievements.

It should not be forgotten that each new member, in 1990, barely contributes with 1,300,000 pesetas (annual wages of wage grade 1), 10% of the capital necessary to acquire the fixed assets subject to the value of the average job. This amount represents, in constant terms, approximately 50% of the 50,000 pesetas contributed in 1960, in relation to the income received by members, which in a third of a century has tripled their purchasing power through payment received for work.

The progressive reduction in capital has been carried out to make the concept of "open admission" more real and there is no direct stimulus to put up a capital stake, especially in terms of profitability. It could be said that the full achievement of the instrumental character of capital in the cooperatives and its subordination to labour, has meant the loss of all types of incentives. This is a fact neutralised only by the profits generated by the business, by the revaluation of assets in the face of inflation and by the financial support which, given the lack of self-financing in certain situations, can be provided by the support bodies, especially the **Intercooperative Solidarity Fund** and **Caja Laboral Popular**.

5. PARTICIPATORY MANAGEMENT

The Mondragón Cooperative Experience believes that the democratic character of the Cooperative is not limited to membership aspects, but that it also implies the progressive development of self-management and consequently of the participation of members in the sphere of business management which, in turn, requires:

a) The development of suitable mechanisms and channels for participation.

b) Freedom of information concerning the development of the basic manage ment variables of the Cooperative.

c) The practice of methods of consultation and negotiation with worker-mebers and their social representatives in economic, organisational and labour decisions which concern or affect them.

d) The systematic application of social and professional training plans for members.

e) The establishment of internal promotion as the basic means of covering posts with greater professional responsibility.

The practice of cooperativism runs counter to the more general and established limited companies, in which primacy lies with those who hold the capital: the more shares they have, the more power they have in running the company.

The challenge with which the cooperatives have been faced in their development - especially worker cooperatives - is derived precisely from their singular nature with respect to those who hold power. The essential character of this difference can be simplified in the following terms:

ooperation brings men together in a collective task, but it gives each one responsibility. It is the development of the individual, not against the rest, but with the rest". (J.M.A.)

- A cooperative is a company made up of people who have equal rights in the management of that company.

- However, the members have different capabilities with respect to the specific knowledge required to understand the internal mechanisms and variables involved for each company, which affects their potential to manage the company in a solvent way.

- The need to take decisions with the dynamism required by a competitive market means that power is concentrated in favour of certain members, who are elected as the most suitable, to facilitate the methodical solution of the problems which arise and the application of the strategies agreed.

- But it should not be forgotten that each and every member wants to manage their company and wants their opinions to be heard, and that companies created with this aim should be self-managed by all the individuals who form them and work in them.

Self-management has to been carried out by means of participation, for which suitable mechanisms and channels must be developed, and it finds in the cooperative, a company conceptually and legally different from that prevailing in self-managed entities, a very affinitive model.

For precisely these reasons, the Cooperatives of the Group decided to allow the management function to permeate as far as possible, without reducing economic efficiency and easing up on competitiveness.

The managers of the cooperatives, be they members of the Governing Council or executives, are faced with the arduous task of reconciling opinions born from different perspectives and which are produced naturally in the spheres in which each member works.

The development of participation necessarily has to be carried out, taking as a basis the knowledge that each member can contribute and is capable of applying in their own sphere of influence, distinguishing two levels of intervention:

- That which each member has to participate in the governing bodies of the cooperative, participating where political power and the control of executive power is exercised, and

- That which members are assigned in the executive structure, for which, at some levels, those who work are given a certain capacity to act freely.

The first level of participation puts all members on an equal basis, and is exercised by members in their capacity as members of the General Assembly, in which the full sovereignty of the cooperative rests. As mentioned previously, in point 2: Democratic Organisation *"the General Assembly, consisting of all the members ... is the supreme body for the expression of the social will"* and some of its non-delegable functions are:

a) To appoint and remove, by secret vote, the members of the Governing Council, Account Auditors and Liquidators.

b) To examine and censure management; approve the accounts and agree on the distribution of profits.

c) To approve the general policies and strategies of the cooperative.

d) To agree on the capital contributions to be made by new members.

e) To approve increases in social capital and the interest to be applied to contributions and the percentage of revaluation.

f) To settle appeals and challenges made with regard to members joining or leaving, expulsions and readmissions and very serious disciplinary proceedings.

g) To approve and modify the Statutes and approve and modify the Internal Regulations.

h) To agree mergers with other cooperatives; and the separation or splitting of the cooperative.

i) Likewise to agree the cession, transfer or sale of centres of work, property or rights, as well as the acquisition, integration or sale of property, rights and activities, the taking of holdings or the establishment and concession of risks with other companies.

j) The promotion of new industrial, commercial or similar activities, which imply a substantial modification in the economic, organisational and functional structure of the cooperative.

k) Where necessary, hold the members of the Governing Council, Management and the Account Auditors accountable.

l) To agree the initiation of the legal steps for the suspension of payments and, where appropriate, for bankruptcy.

m) Agree the dissolution of the cooperative, the appointment and cessation of liquidators, and to approve liquidation.

The **Governing Council** is elected by all the members and its members carry out their functions with the care required in their capacity as representatives of the rest of the members. They are responsible for damage to the corporate assets due to malice, misuse of powers or serious negligence.

Subordinate to the policies established by the General Assembly the Council has, amongst others, the following responsibilities:

a) To reach agreement on all matters related to members joining and leaving.

b) To represent the cooperative, by delegation, in any type of acts or contracts.

c) To appoint the managing director and the top management of the cooperative.

d) To decide the work and disciplinary system for members, their professional classification, the organisation of work and the amount of wages paid.

e) To propose modifications to the General Assembly in the Statutes and Internal Regulations.

f) To carry out acts and sign contracts necessary to fulfil the authorised activities, even in credit operations and guarantees.

g) To define the specific application of the Social Welfare Fund.

h) Annually at the General Assembly, to produce the accounts, balance sheet and annual report of the cooperative, and

i) To settle any doubts which may arise as to the interpretation of the cooperative's Statutes.

Ensuring, however, that social or policy matters are controlled in this way does not mean that the level of participation corresponding to members is obtained. The fact is that the concept of self-management does not naturally arise from control of the cooperative through the systematic application of its precepts.

However, in all the cooperatives of the Group, it is general practice to draw up a document known as the Annual Management Plan. This is the way in which, before the start of each economic year, the management model which it is intended to follow is controlled.

This Plan is **farsighted**, in that it evaluates the policies to be applied in the cooperative to gain an adequate position in the market; it is **participatory**, to the extent that it should include the technical, marketing, economic, financial and social aspirations in relation with the working community, in which any request from executive management may appear, although, in the last instance it is the Governing Council and General Assembly which approve it; and it is a **social control** mechanism, through which daily management is systematically compared with the forecasts which Management had established amongst the options formulated, so that initial responsibility for compliance rests with the executive management.

The Annual Management Plan must in turn conform to a longer term Strategic Plan, which is necessary if one takes into account that the cycles companies require to develop their programmes extend beyond the limited annual horizon.

Both documents - remember function c) of the General Assembly - are subject in their essential points to the approval of this General Assembly.

In more practical terms, a constant preoccupation in the Group has been the application of *"new ways of organising work"* which respond to the personal interest of the members in increasing the professional content of their jobs. The tasks to be assumed are decided by the **work group** depending on the characteristics of its members, and after negotiation with executive management, the work to be carried out by the group is self-managed.

The Management Plan in close relation with the participatory management by objectives which has been established therein, and the new ways of organising work, are the mechanisms which give the cooperativism of the Group a certain originality in the labour sphere in which it operates. In any case, the Group's organisational culture is a faithful part of the general conduct of the cooperative companies which form it.

Freedom of information is governed by the members' right to information, which enables them to request in writing or verbally any clarification they may require. The General Assembly must reply, verbally if possible at the Assembly itself, or as soon as practically possible. Outside the General Assembly, the Governing Council must reply in thirty days, to any question raised by ten percent of the members.

Organically, the Social Council, on at least a quarterly basis, must be informed on the development of the cooperative and on matters required of it.

The methods of consultation are thus established, with a body specific to the Group standing out: the **Social Council**, which is not envisaged in current legislation.

Its members are elected democratically in the work centres of the cooperative. It meets at least once a month to carry out its functions through information, advice and negotiation with the Governing Council, and exercises control over social aspects or matters which affect the members as workers. It draws up proposals on the policies of the cooperative, participating in the bodies in which it has representatives, answering queries put to it and informing those it represents.

In its **advisory and information** role, it informs or reports on the policy and aims of the Management Plans, selection criteria for new members, matters related to the training and promotion of members, evaluation and classification of jobs, regulations dealing with payment and the working day, regulations on changes of job and working conditions, norms for strikes for external reasons, social security and company medicine matters, control of new organisational changes derived from plant reorganisation and reconversions, statutory regulations, and any procedures which are followed to facilitate communication with, and the participation of, members.

The **negotiation** function covers those matters which cause conflict between staff and Management of a general nature or if they only affect one collective. Negotiable matters are dealt with separately from those which have been defined as falling under the heading of consultation and information.

As far as **social control** is concerned it is the Social Council's task to ensure compliance with the agreements adopted in the bodies of the cooperative and in particular, in line with the objectives of the Management and Strategic Plans, with the technical support and additional information obtained from the President or the Management of the Cooperative.

The support mechanisms for **social and professional training** are stimulated by the application of an internal policy and by external events which suggest the need for updating personnel on new management methods. The Eskola Politeknikoa, special courses, the Otalora Centre, trips and freedom of information, constitute a package of opportunities whose cost is not less than 3% of the total payroll. It could also be said that the Education and Social Welfare fund plays a role here which is both cooperative and necessary.

Internal promotion is a mechanism which has been used systematically from the start of the Cooperative Experience. It is based on the emergence of needs which were always best met by turning to members immersed in cooperative culture, not just because they would understand its singular nature, but also because they would live in a cooperative fashion with the personal renunciations and satisfactions which the assumption of such a mission entails.

Promotion in the executive branch is entrusted to Management. However, given the strict social controls and constantly monitored requirements to achieve satisfactory results, management should set its priorities with objectivity and impartiality.

6. PAYMENT SOLIDARITY

The Mondragón Cooperative Experience proclaims sufficient and solidary remuneration to be a basic principle in its management, expressed in the following terms:

a) Sufficient, in accordance with the possibilities of the Cooperative

b) Solidary, in the following specific spheres:

— Internal. Materialised, amongst other aspects, in the existence of a differential, based on solidarity, in payment for work.

— External. Materialised in the criteria that average internal payment levels are equivalent to those of salaried workers in the area, unless the wage policy in this area is obviously insufficient.

Probably in the origin of the Cooperative *Experience*, amongst the motives which inspired it, apart from the change in structure, there was the reduction of the gap in the enjoyment of the wealth generated by work.

The payment differential in companies was enormous and discriminatory and, what is worse, salaries were insufficient at lower levels, with the result that workers had to live in want.

In these circumstances payment solidarity gave priority, over any other formulation or scope of application of the concept, to sharing in the needs of others. This was an attempt to create a new company model whose ideological, and consequently legal, structures, prevented the establishment of paternalistic criteria, thereby giving an unalienable right to labour, over any other factor integrated in the cooperative.

"A constant in cooperativism, both theoretical and practical, is solidarity". (J.M.A.)

164

The wage differential of 1 to 3 between the worker-member in posts generating little value added, and the managing director, who supposedly had the most valuable and remunerable job, was a decisive step in staving off any sign of social outrage at the distribution of the wealth generated. It became a symbol and lasted more than 20 years. The first alterations to this rigorous two pronged system came as a result of a widening of the responsibilities of top management, due to the growth in the activities of the cooperatives which exceeded the expectations of the most optimistic of their promoters.

Simultaneously the growth in available income increased at all levels, accelerating at a higher rate than the consumer price index. This meant members now had general access to other things, which were previously beyond their reach, such as university educations, their own homes and domestic appliances and a car.

In this climate of social recovery, it was proposed that a complementary index be adopted. This was called the "labour compensation bonus" and its aim was to improve the remuneration of those managers with most responsibility, in relation to the effort required and the number of extra hours worked, which were not paid by the cooperative, and for the exclusive and committed dedication in carrying out their functions. This "bonus" continued to grow in light of the new situation in which society was wealthier and companies bigger and more complex, until by 1976 the maximum "compensation bonus" was 50% on top of the nominal upper limit of grade 3.

At this time the average salary grade for all members had risen from 1.4 to 1.65, in an relentless increase in the aspirations of worker-members, be it due to the establishment of the seniority bonus, to the greater complexity of each job, or to simple adaptations to the evaluation manuals. The latter were updated from time to time and this always resulted in an increase in the average salary grade, a necessary sociological cost to meet with general approval.

Finally at the end of 1987 and the start of 1988, the 1st Cooperative Congress approved the basic Regulations on the Wage Differential in the Cooperative Group which stated that *"the maximum received, on an annual basis, by a worker-member cannot exceed a total corresponding to salary grade 6 ... (including) all wage components, structural factor, functional factor, seniority bonus, or any other application in accordance with the payment or evaluation regulations applied in each cooperative"*.

This is the limit currently in force and, consequently, the wage differential has gone from a maximum limit of 3 to 6. However, it is not rigorously so, as from 1979, eleven years ago, each member started to pay Income Tax directly, instead of the cooperative doing it for him.

In this change of system all members received the same percentage increase (11.6%), which was equivalent to the average deduction for the whole workforce. At present tax deductions (everybody also makes a tax declaration every year) for members on salary grade one, with two children is 5% of gross income, whilst for those on grade six it is 32%. So the practical relationship of *"income available for consumption"* is equivalent to grade 4.08 and 0.95 for the minimum - in terms comparable to 1956 when the payment differential was created.

Between these extremes the final differential is 4.29, which is the figure which should really be compared with the original figure of 3. So the degree of solidarity is rigorously established. This was a symbol which at the start of the *Experience* caught people's attention as evidence of the will of the founders to reduce social class differences by restricting their wages to a level clearly lower than the average.

It can never be demonstrated whether payment levels have been established objectively. More income creates more needs and as society gradually enters new spheres of culture, social wellbeing, has access to more possibilities and options in life, needs increase in an unlimited way. But a basis has to be found to establish levels of payment and in our *Experience* the following two references are used:

The first is based on the possibilities allowed by the economic performance of the cooperative. With splendid results, taking advantage of the peaks in economic cycles, some cooperatives are unable to resist earmarking part of the surplus generated in the form of advance payments (wages), over and above the average for the Group.

On the other hand, those companies obliged to reduce costs to try to get into profit, tend to reduce the wage bill. To try to bring these two extremes closer together, the 2nd Congress of the Mondragon Cooperative Group held on 1st and 2nd December 1989 passed a resolution on Intercooperative Solidarity in the Application of the Basic Concepts of the Labour System, which defined that the extremes would be kept between 90% and 110% of the average wages calculated annually by Lagun-Aro, to establish benefits and contributions. In this way, with this wide range of approximately 20%, guidelines are established which, in terms of gross annual payments, the companies can neither exceed nor fall short of.

The second reference is based on the average salaries in the area, *"unless these are clearly insufficient"*, to which end *"every three years the difference between the advance payments (wages) of the Group and the salaries of the Iron and Steel Industry shall be appraised"* ... *"by means of a comparative study of payments made under social control"*.

With both references, every year the cooperative's possibilities for increasing the wages of all members in the same proportion are studied. There is also a degree of upgrading each year, either due to the automatic application of a seniority bonus, or to professional promotion carried out *"in accordance with the abilities of each member and their professional capabilities"*.

The statistical data confirms that, after thirty four years of having experienced practical cooperativism, the purchasing power of members has been multiplied by two and a half. In other words, in 1990 a member with salary grade 1 (the minimum) has the purchasing power of management in 1956, with a salary grade then of 2.5.

In terms of the hourly wage, in the thirty year period from 1960 to 1990 it has been multiplied by 63.3 whilst the Consumer Price Index has been multiplied by 18.

The number of hours worked annually has fallen from 2,760 in 1956 to 1,780 in 1990. In short, members are now working 64% of the time they worked at the start of the Experience, and over this period the minimum salary has increased its purchasing power to the equivalent of grade 2.5 in 1956. But these advantages have taken place in all of society, because on the basis of *"the average internal wage shall be equivalent to that of local salaried workers"* the Group has maintained genuine solidarity with those around it and has protected itself through self-financing in order to participate in the spread of the Cooperative *Experience*.

The concept of payment, in spite of its long history in the complex and sour trajectory of labour relations, is always a tense subject which is practically impossible to resolve through an efficient mechanism capable of automatically defining increases in wages. Only a systematic delving into the ethical concepts which surround cooperative principles, and the individual renunciation of self-enrichment, are spiritual and not material hurdles, capable of keeping the members of the cooperatives within the limits of payment solidarity, in relation to the development of their own cooperative, and in line with the average outside the Group. Cooperators have excellent opportunities for self-management, and can turn to the General Assembly to decide, if they so wish, a fair increase in their wages. Only intelligent participation in the destiny of their company limits the little room for manoeuvre that there is between labour costs close to 25% of the value of sales and the menacing field of competitiveness.

It should be understood that payment solidarity is exercised to keep at bay the temptation to establish classes as the fundamental guidelines in the structural reform which Mondragon cooperativism wanted to make.

The sociological extremes of this solidarity are: the minimum payment limit for members in the most skilled jobs, without breaking their adhesion to the system, and the profitability of the cooperatives, which, if wages were based on the desire to earn more money, would go bankrupt, as this would go beyond a profitability capable of keeping the company alive forever through collective savings in solidarity with the rest.

The words of Don José María Arizmendiarrieta should not be forgotten: *"Knowledge democratises power"*. So the general and positive development of access to knowledge tends to establish more comparable levels of remuneration as an inevitable contribution of democratisation. On the other hand, now that the period of extreme shortages and poverty has been overcome, the payment range is no longer a decisive nor basic symbol of solidarity. This does prevent the distribution of the wealth created from being just and freedom of information from standing out as evidence of unextinguishable participative democracy.

As the founder of the cooperative experience, Don José María Arizmendiarrieta, said: *"Solidarity is not just a theoretical proclamation, but something that should be put into practice and made manifest, willingly accepting the limitations of team work and of association, since this is the way to enable people to help each other"*.

7. INTERCOOPERATION

The *Mondragón Cooperative Experience* considers that, as a specific application of solidarity and a requirement for business efficiency, the principle of Intercooperation should be evident:

a) Between individual Cooperatives, through the creation of Groupings ten ding towards the establishment of a homogeneous socio-labour system, inclu ding the pooling of profits, controlled transfer of worker-members and the search for potential synergies derived from their combined size.

b) Between Groupings, by means of the democratic constitution and management, for the common good, of support entities and bodies.

c) Between the *Mondragon Cooperative Experience* and other Basque cooperative organisations, in order to promote the Basque Cooperative Movement.

d) With other cooperative movements in Spain, Europe and the rest of the world, making agreements and setting up joint bodies aimed at stimulating development.

66

It is a risk to make each cooperative a closed world. We must consider intercooperative solidarity the only resource to be used to forestall other problems of growth and maturity: we must consider a growing development adapted to circumstance". (J.M.A.)

Intercooperation is a very wide concept aimed at examining the degree of cooperation which the Cooperative Group exercises at its heart and in the sphere of relations with other cooperatives; in short, it is a matter of cooperating with cooperatives.

The mechanisms for collaboration have been driven at different times by different stimuli and the sustained development achieved by the Group is the most faithful reflection of this drive for intercooperation.

The history of the Group itself, starting with the Eskola Politeknikoa in 1943, the creation of the first cooperatives 12 years later in 1955, by five of its students, and the establishment of Lagun-Aro and Caja Laboral Popular, as support and coordinating bodies, are in effect achievements which demonstrate the degree of intercooperation maintained by the *Experience*.

However, this model of collaboration and grouping has had limits. Not so much in terms of internal development, but in its relations with institutions or plans for intercooperation proposed from outside. For this reason it is best to examine "intercooperation" from these two standpoints.

Internal Intercooperation

Whenever we speak of intercooperation, we do so with two parties in mind. The main party, the best situated in terms of potential, is that which should act for the benefit of another. In the Group this party was first Ulgor, the cooperative created in 1955, and later Caja Laboral Popular. They spread their operating model and gave decisive support locally, in an area in which they in turn could count on the support of specialists and professionals who had studied in the Eskola Politeknikoa, also a cooperative. Thorough the collaboration of Ulgor, (whose trademark was Fagor), Arrasate, Copreci, Ederlan, Soraluce, Enara, Ulma, Lana, Lagun-Aro and Caja Laboral Popular were created; and all this in the first ten years of the Experience begun in Vitoria. The business criteria was based on the development of complementary programmes, extending production support, generating employment to exchange workers in crisis situations, and on obtaining economies insofar as certain representation, promotion and long term development work could, in an intercooperative fashion, be given to a mutual support body.

Caja Laboral Popular and Lagun-Aro became, in their own right, the authentic promoters of intercooperation, with the specific tasks of ensuring the financing of the development aspired to and of creating a singular social welfare cover for cooperative members, in their capacity as self-employed workers. Ulgor played an extremely important role at that time, a period, strongly marked by idealism, in which ethical concepts driven by a wave of economic success prevailed.

For this reason when Ulgor decided to take on the task of expansion and the promotion of new initiatives, ignoring its pre-eminent position in which it had 80% of the human, financial and technological potential achieved by the *Cooperative Experience* by 1959, it provided a great service to intercooperation.

Having created new cooperatives in the surrounding area, on 1st January 1965 a Local Cooperative Group known as Ularco was created. This Group was made up of the following cooperatives: Ulgor, Arrasate, Copreci, Ederlan and Fagelectro. Ularco was also a private institution, not officially registered, which pragmatically took on the functions which had, in fact, been carried out by Ulgor in preceding years.

The sense of local intercooperation responded to the desire to overcome insufficient individual size for tackling functions which can and should be shared, to generate:

Socio-economic development of the Area or Region,

- A common cooperative staffing policy,

- The establishment of solidarity in economic, financial and human aspects.

- The planning of harmonious development in the Area or Region,

- The pooling of central services to reduce structural costs.

Intercooperation was later extended to other areas of the Basque Country and, 20 years later, there were 17 Groups (including Eroski, the consumer group, and Hezibide, the educational group).

In 1983, when there was more competition and the idea of the Single European Market was more than a mere plan, work began on developing the concept of **groupings based on technological sectors**.

Just as the social projects are the same for all types of cooperative activity, and that the answer lies in intercooperation by areas or geographical zones, the type of activity, especially industrial, in worker cooperatives, is organised on the basis of technological homogeneity through the strengthening of marketing, industrial reconversion, innovation and research functions.

The concept of intercooperation which from 1983 onwards was the subject of much reflection in the Mondragon Cooperative Group was aimed at:

1. Realigning production programmes,
2. Creating specialised R + D centres,
3. Unifying trade names,

4. Establishing joint relations at international level,

5. Carrying out joint strategies,

6. Creating a policy of industrial development

The result of all these hypotheses was the creation of the Congress of the Mondragon Cooperative Group at the end of 1984. This clearly demonstrated the concerns that there were with regard to intercooperation, and united all the cooperatives associated with Caja Laboral Popular in a programme dealing with the *"maintenance, perfection and promotion of the essence of our Cooperative Experience"*. The principal role which Caja Laboral Popular had played up to that point, perhaps exceeding its functions, having taken over the promotion of intercooperation from Ulgor in 1965, was now taken by the Congress. A democratic forum consisting of 350 members was therefore created, to develop the essence of intercooperation.

On the same date the General Council was created, made up of all the General Managers of the cooperative groups *"as a intercooperative executive, coordinating and arbitration body"*, the clear forerunner of the executive body of the Mondragon Cooperative Group, based, now, on the framework of sectorial groups.

In any case, there is an essential latent element of solidarity in the very concept of intercooperation.

It is difficult to create intercooperative links based only on ethical concepts emanating from cooperative principles. In the last analysis, every cooperative could become a shielded world operating alone in an open and competitive market. Although such small-mindedness would in the long term present the danger of numbness and senility, badly managed and planned communities, have a short term vision which is incapable of exercising intercooperation based on solidarity, and of seeing that this bears fruit in the longer term.

But it is obvious that solidarity, the essential seed of intercooperation, can only occur when one of the protagonists is capable of giving up some of his rights and privileges infavour of the rest. Intercooperation is never possible when everyone comes together to practice it by trying to obtain immediate and short term results. The situation depends on the companies, and the external effects are different at different times. It is clear that in the capitalist world groups and large corporations have in their size and unified management,due to the combination of various factors capable of compensating these situations, the best support for their solidity and stability. It can be said that capitalism is not magnanimous when it comes to distributing wealth but it cannot be denied that it has the pragmatism necessary to perpetuate itself by reducing risks and gaining ascendancy.

External Intercooperation

The intercooperation of the Mondragon Cooperative Group with other cooperative organisations followed a practical process in the way it was carried out and developed.

The absence of the Consejo Superior de Cooperativas, which was created in 1983, prevented the establishment of institutional links which were not based on setting up a private individual model.

The *Cooperative Experience* was open to any cooperative company which wished to associate with Caja Laboral Popular and Lagun-Aro, from 1960 onwards. The resulting associations from Irun to Baracaldo and from the Urola Valley to Estella, are clear evidence of this attitude.

Difficulties in developing a vigorous plan for intercooperation generally arose for three reasons:

- Firstly, there were cooperatives whose methods of operation were not based on the principle of freedom of information, or who did not allow all their workers to become members, taking on employed workers, who had pay differentials higher than those fixed by the Group or, who, in the last analysis, were badly managed. Often the latter, and not any ideological reasons, was why such cooperatives wanted to join the Group, becoming members of Caja Laboral Popular and Lagun- Aro, as a last resort to solve their critical situation.

- On other occasions the cooperatives would decide not to "intercooperate" with the Group as they felt more protected in isolation, developing a life of their own. This has normally occurred with strong cooperatives, who thought that any strategic move, in relation to the Group, could change the excellent performance of their company, of which they would lose some control. The final decision was always conditioned by top management, and the way they formulated the proposal affected the result in the General Assembly.

- The third difficulty arose when the cooperatives associated with Caja Laboral Popular began to favour the idea of advancing towards an industrial group. From this standpoint it was best that certain cooperatives joined right away the sectors on offer, which had already been selected by the Group as part of its strategy for development and consolidation. The incompatibilities that could arise discouraged some cooperatives from joining, when it was proposed that they accept intercooperative regulations.

In any case, in the Basque Cooperative Movement, there were never an excessive number of cooperatives with whom to intercooperate either due to size or the reason for their creation or attitude. It could be said that, between 1960 and 1975, the tendency of the Group was to make a big effort, via Caja Laboral Popular and based on the organizational model of the Ularco Group, to take on more cooperatives.

These were times in which the intercooperation of the Group, going beyond these limits, took part in the conversion of limited companies into cooperatives. Coinma, Orbea, Irizar, Ederlan, Urola and later Radar, are examples which come to mind.

Now, thanks to participation in the Consejo Superior de Cooperativas, financing through Caja Laboral Popular has progressed and the courses held in Ikasbide-Otalora are the first symptoms of a positive and stable development in intercooperation with cooperatives outside the Mondragón Cooperative Group.

As relations spread further afield, the repercussions are fewer. In any case, collaboration is extensive, although not as solid and committed as might be expected with cooperatives in the rest of Spain.

The protagonists of the *Experience,* either institutions or people, have always been prepared to collaborate in drawing up legislation and regulations. There are examples of intercooperation which should be strengthened further in Catalonia, Andalusia, Valencia, as should those with any other initiative in which the initial steps are taken in a responsible fashion by the cooperatives in question. Possibilities of collaboration and intercooperation have never been denied to these.

It would of course also be gratifying to be able to extend this to other countries.

8. SOCIAL TRANSFORMATION

The *Mondragon Cooperative Experience* manifests its desire for social transformation based on solidarity with that of other peoples, through its activities in the Basque Country in a process of expansion which will contribute to economic and social reconstruction and to the creation of a Basque society which is more free, just and solidary, by means of:

(a) The reinvestment of the greater part of the Net Profits obtained, earmarking a significant proportion to Funds of a community nature, to enable the creation of new jobs in the cooperative system.

(b) The support for community development initiatives, through the application of the Social Welfare Fund.

(c) A Social Security policy coherent with the cooperative system, based on solidarity and responsibility.

(d) Cooperation with other Basque institutions of an economic and social nature, especially those promoted by the Basque working class.

(e) Collaboration of the recovery of Basque as the national language and, in general, of elements characteristic of Basque culture.

"T*he economic and social process, which shapes a new social order; cooperators should converge together on this final aim with all those who hunger and thirst for justice in the labour world". (J.M.A.)*

Without faltering on the principle of intercooperation mention should also be made of the social experience developed by the Mondragon Cooperative, working in favour of social emancipation in the framework of the Basque Country.

The main obligations of the *Cooperative Experience* lie in the area where it first sprang forth, where the provinces of Guipúzcoa, Vizcaya and Alava meet, in Mondragón, on the slopes of Besaide.

The instinct for development was guided along the road to structural change, in a modest attempt to achieve social transformation in the spheres of work, consumption, credit, education, social security, research and housing. The principle of transformation declared, always referred more to a setting whose most cultivated reference point was the Eskola Politeknikoa than to the cooperative centres of work themselves. The spread of cooperativism was carried out to a great extent by the students of the School, which, as it gained prestige, accepted those students whose family and social life were to be found in nearby towns in the Basque Country. Don José María Arizmendiarrieta, dedicated above all to the parish church and to "his School", imparted a message which had in him its greatest influence. He probably never directly gave his students access to specifically cooperative disciplines and yet, when, convinced he was right, he used to say *"The only thing capitalist companies can offer you is more money"*, he was transmitting an idea of which his students were scarcely aware, by indicating that cooperativism was a model for companies more likely to guarantee greater immaterial satisfaction for their spirits.

His advice always came up against initial indifference, because to understand him in his hypotheses integrating *"man in the economic and social process, which is shaping a new order"* meant having the same degree of sensitivity, perception and intelligence.

Here, in this sphere, emanating outwards, the Mondragon *Cooperative Experience* was born, but it has spread no further, in the form of specific accomplishments, than it was possible for the unceasing teaching of the founder of the Experience to spread.

Guided by the same aspirations, there is a certain element which the Cooperative Group has developed as a culture submerged in its roots. The contributions to the Education and Welfare Funds (10% of profits) were never used for the benefit of the members of the cooperatives which produced them. It was understood, and still is, that these funds were for financing activities outside the cooperative itself, and for providing other non-profit making cooperatives, mainly educational, with funds for cultural purposes.

However, it has been the 50% of profits earmarked for compulsory funds and non-distributable reserves, which has uninterruptedly served to spread cooperativism over the length and breadth of the Basque Country. This was due to a policy which can be explained, if necessary, by the following essential factors:

- Robust cooperativism, that which encourages commitment, is that which is clothed in the experience of those who found the cooperative, who unequivocally have a desire for social emancipation; not to have experience in order to promote a change in one's status of dependence on others is a dead weight when it comes to understanding cooperativism as a legal form for governing a company.

- The cooperative seed must be protected if in its germination and growing phase there are not to be upsets in its organic structure, derived from its ideological model, nor operational errors as a company under siege from the competition. Proximity is a necessary condition for the rearing of new cooperatives.

- The phenomena of intercooperation have very sensitive ingredients which have to be arrived at through common, homogenous assumptions by those who found the cooperative. These ingredients have to be based on ethical concepts, born in the heat of the love for the earth in which they live, for the concepts of political or religious idealism, or for simple similarities which arise from the conviction that work humanises man *"who becomes whole when he has control of the instrument of his labour"*. The balancing of these ideas, which come from the spirit and are far removed from a desire for profit, constitutes the basis for the spread of the cooperative fervour of Mondragon over the whole of the Basque Country.

With these attributes as the starting point, the intercooperative mark has been stamped in cooperatives which personify the *Experience* to the very end.

Lagun-Aro, one of Caja Laboral Popular's activities at the start (1959-1967), was created, as has been explained, to solve the precarious situation in which the members of the cooperatives found themselves when they were excluded from the part of the Social Security System for employed workers. However, rather than tackling this situation as a brunt to be borne, it has served to strengthen the cooperative nature of the members of the *Experience.*

The Social Security System, administered by the State, establishes a necessarily protective cover which is practically universally available and therefore based on the limitations of contributions and the Budget, as another form of income redistribution. Those who pay contributions in no way feel themselves to be owners of the system, nor do those who receive benefits feel any responsibility for the expense, because the relationship is based on mechanisms which make people think that the Social Security System belongs to the State and there is a permanent temptation towards the attitude of getting the most out of it as possible.

In harmony with the cooperative system, the Social Security System implemented in the Group through Lagun-Aro establishes formulas which motivate a sense of saving in the provision of benefits; of a balance between the contributions paid and the quality of the services received; of freedom of information, which must be reiterated, timely, regular and democratic, when it comes to electing the Governing Council, which is to administer the System.

The results do credit to the members who are obliged, on the basis of prudence, solidarity and responsibility, to consider human issues, and greater savings, better services and greater accessibility in order to improve, progressively, the benefits, from the economic point of view.

It has not been difficult to maintain a neighbourly policy with other Basque worker movements: unions. The truth is that the origins of Mondragon cooperativism lay in the unceasing search for solutions to remedy the eternal subordination of labour to capital and the permanent tension which abounds when it comes to distributing the wealth generated, through the transformation of structures to modify sovereignty.

The promoters of the experience participated in the "illegal" strikes of the period 1950 - 1955 (when the first cooperative was created), although it was not because these demonstrations of disagreement were prohibited that they decided to create the cooperatives.

Their aspirations were based on the desire to find a solution to overcome the class struggle and the need for conflict, through a change in the attitude of the forces set against each other. For this to be possible, the workers also had to be owners, in a situation in which they saw the company as their own, without feeling alienated from their jobs and the room for manoeuvre which they have in their capacity as those who provide all the effort.

It is not difficult to see the parallels between unions and cooperativism. In cooperativism conflicts are overcome by giving the worker-members the right to call a General Assembly with 20% of votes. This can be achieved in their capacity as *"the supreme body for the expression of the social will"* when the workers think it necessary. The Assembly can raise wages, reduce hours, replace management, be they members of the Governing Council or the managing director, and impose any organizational model they require. This attitude is based on the recognition that the workers are mature and have the right to emancipation, freeing themselves from the servitude to which they were subject through contracts signed with the owners of private companies, to which they offered their labour and intelligence.

The option of all members to exercise their sovereignty at any time is their alternative to conflictive disagreement. The labour contract, which is replaced by a membership contract, means that the worker is a member and self-employed worker instead of an employed worker. The union, an irreplaceable weapon for salaried workers, should be encountered in the cooperatives when there are disagreements with the worker-owners of the company, that is to say, with themselves, as those who work in the cooperative can decide on all matters affecting their company in the General Assembly.

The identity of the Basque Country through its language and culture can be clearly seen in the application of the Education and Welfare Fund, in striving for identification in its administration mechanisms, in the spread of its message in all documents and, above all, in the sensitivity of its people in their identification with the problems of their region. There is something substantial in the Basque Country which made it possible for the Experience to be born, with perfect assimilation of the human values rooted in the climate which gave it substance and basis.

9. UNIVERSALITY

The *Mondragon Cooperative Experience,* as an expression of its universality, proclaims its solidarity with all those working for economic democracy in the sphere of the "Social Economy", championing the objectives of Peace, Justice and Development, which are essential features of International Cooperativism.

The Mondragon Cooperative's Group approximation to principles of universality has occurred as it developed in size and potential, and as coexistence with other initiatives enabled it to share experiences and a sense of affinity.

When the first company was created and transformed into a cooperative after three years, the pionneers of Mondragon did not study international cooperativism, nor even other models with which their aspirations might have been related, because their aims were simply centred on creating an example of a company in which the workers were in turn entrepreneurs in a democratic organisation. This was the road they thought necessary to ensure possible justice.

Having achieved development by extending its activities and establishing ties of intercooperation, the Experience took on density and began to be studied from outside, especially from the English-speaking world. These academics placed the Mondragon Cooperative Group amongst those companies which offered a social example, due to the success achieved through worker cooperativism.

*othing about man surprises me, said the pre- Christian philosopher. An honourable man should be ashamed of being, and living like, a rich man in a world of 2,000 million undernourished people".* (J.M.A.)

The Mondragon Cooperative Group is now a member of CICOPA and EUROCOOP and the Basque Federations of Worker, Consumer, Educational, Credit and Agricultural Cooperatives which together form the Consejo Superior de Cooperativas. This opening up, insofar as it can be useful, is in harmony with its intercooperative vocation.

The Group's solidarity with those who work for economic democracy comes from its own roots. Don José María Arizmendiarrieta said at the start of the Experience. *"we should be concerned with those who form the legion of labour and who hope to progress and transform profoundly their structures. A whole economic world for those who need the force that we can offer in economic and financial plans"* *"our contribution to the labour cause, at this moment and as a real demonstration of solidarity, is to show the world"*.

The Social Economy, although not well defined in Spain, but subjectively situated close to democratically organised companies and to those in which the workers exercise maximum social rights, has for the last twelve years been expanding. The reason for this lies in the negative results obtained by companies in the face of the successive oil crises in the 70's. The current protagonists of the Social Economy worked in these companies and had to take charge of them to save their jobs. The tendency has been more towards the creation of Sociedades Anonimas Laborales (SAL's)[1], as these were easier to set up, by transferring the shares of the old owners to the workers. The creation of cooperatives was more difficult, because it was first necessary to found the cooperative and then later purchase the company in its name.

The precarious nature of the situation and the tension created in companies with no clear future has meant that more workers have turned their companies into SAL's rather than establishing new cooperatives in the last few years.

The values of intercooperation, democracy, justice and a fair distribution of wealth, are factors which are themselves capable of establishing universality.

The *Experience* is known in South America, by academics in the United States and by companies which have worker participation.

For many years we have been developing a policy of maintaining such relations, respecting the fact that the principal role must be left to those involved in each country.

On this basis the *Experience* has cooperated with the Soviet Union by making available the legal documents describing the organizational model of the Mondragon Cooperative Group to its Ambassador in Madrid, Mr Romanovski, who passed them on to Prime Minister Rizhkov. Visits made to the Soviet Union have always been based on principles of Peace and

(1) Companies in which at least 51% of the shares are in the hands of the workers.

Justice, and relations have also been developed according to the possibilities that a Group, which when all is said and done is rather limited, can offer.

Otalora-Ikasbide is the means provided by the Group to develop these objectives and its support, never sufficient however generous it may be, will be felt above all through technical and collaborative training in the launching of worker initiatives in countries prepared to take on such an endeavour.

However the practical result achievable should not be exaggerated, because, in universal terms, the Experience has a testimonial value.

What can be asserted is the desire of the *Experience* to work towards the unlimited development of the system, permanently strengthening the legacy of its own companies and initiatives.

Probably the most important task at this time is to develop an effective policy to ensure that the substantial change in political variables does not affect organisational strategies. After establishing the new ideas necessary to maintain the same vigour in a more aggressive and competitive environment, let us hope that is possible to maintain the same scale of ethical values with which the Experience was born.

It would be nice to be able to say, if this were to occur, remembering the words of Juvenal, that *"we live because the reasons for living are still there"*, although the circumstances which form the competitive framework, and its financial and political imperatives, make the universality which the Mondragon Cooperative Group has experienced over the last 35 years inviable.

The proclamation that the Mondragon Cooperative Group makes of Peace, Justice and Social Development is a conscious result of its assumption of democracy in the control of its companies, and of justice in the distribution of the wealth generated thanks to work. These are precepts adopted by International Cooperativism and by all people, men and women, who are free.

10. EDUCATION

The *Mondragon Cooperative Experience* manifests that to promote the implantation of these Principles it is essential that sufficient human and economic resources be provided for Education, in its various aspects:

a)   Cooperative, for all members and especially those elected to office in the social bodies.

b)   Professional, especially for members appointed to management bodies.

c)   In general, of youth, to encourage the emergence of new cooperators, capable of consolidating and developing the Experience in the future.

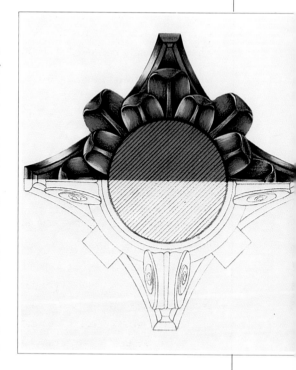

Probably if society in general were saturated with cooperativism, the basic principle which establishes education as the vehicle for maintaining the freshness of its message in companies created would never have arisen. The uninterrupted exchange of experiences and daily coexistence with cooperative ideals would be sufficient.

But it is not cooperative culture which prevails in society. The prevailing culture is related to historic events, economic cycles, the political model in force, the level of education acquired and the effects of other religious or ethical factors, which in turn are all affected by the different strata into which society is divided, on the basis of origin or economic capacity.

Cooperativism has to struggle in a somewhat obstinate fashion if it wants to survive, because the precepts emanating from its principles are not in common use.

It has been said that cooperativism is an economic movement which utilises educational activities, bu this definition could be changed to state that it is an educational movement which utilises economic activities". (J.M.A.)

The democratic control of companies, the limited interest paid on capital with no political power, and the distribution of profits on the basis of the service provided, and not of the capital risked, are key principles which run counter to the common model of behaviour followed by societies and people on the basis of a rough interpretation of the values which provide wellbeing.

Cooperative education therefore emerges as a defence of its own identity, determined that the social model which arises from its principles shall not be erased by the insensitive penetration of other forms of social behaviour in which profit is the central motive.

It is a hypothesis of the International Cooperative Alliance that *"the effort to give the economic system a new force, based on Cooperative Principles, requires a form of discipline different from that normal in individual companies or in government circles"* ... *"it is a force of mutual aid, which is driven by motives different from those based on egotism and personal interest"* ... *"discipline freely tolerated by a collective is not produced or propagated spontaneously: it has to be cultivated"*.

In the Mondragon Cooperative Group the message of Don José Maria Arizmendiarrieta was basic, especially whe coined the idea that *"education is the natural and indispensable nexus of support for the promotion of a new social, human and just order"*, and *"the company is the main social-economic cell and in it we have to establish the fundamental relationship between labour and capital, so that people, that is to say, human capital, are not just the most important driving force behind the economy, but its aim as well"* (since) ... *"Companies are created by men: men with technical and moral capabilities"*.

Bearing this in mind the Statutes and Regulations of the Cooperatives in the Group are quite imperative when stating ... *"the Cooperative should make it possible for its members to raise their professional level in tune with their capabilities"* and for them to receive *"professional retraining necessary by way of compensation for the harm caused them in their professional development"* ... *"The training of members shall be mainly provided through work experience and participation in channels of information and social bodies. However, the cooperative shall organise courses, seminars and any other training activities necessary to complete this training"*.

From the point of view of applying specific measures to put these aspirations into practice the standard Regulations of the cooperatives state:

"The Cooperative is specifically obliged to: earmark a significant amount for the financing of training activities for members; facilitate members' attendance of educational activities and courses by giving training leave, paid or not, for the cases and under the conditions specified; and finally organise, when necessary, its own training activities".

However, it is clear that the concept of training applied here puts more emphasis on vocational training to improve the members' capabilities with respect to their job than on cooperative training. It was thought that the prolific and profound teachings of the founder Don José María Arizmendiarrieta were an inexhaustible source and that subsequently, practising cooperativism itself as the next thing closest.

But this is not sufficient. As materialist values began to play a larger role in human convictions, the Group foresaw a weakening of its ideological support, if it were only to be based on pragmatic values. It saw a need therefore to make a sustained effort to channel cooperative education through the best means possible.

So in 1984, with the support of Caja Laboral Popular, the Ikasbide-Otalora Training Centre was created. Education and the spread of cooperativism are its main activities.

It functions were established admitting that cooperativism *is a higher stage in social relations between the basic sectors which make up the company, which means a greater level of complexity and, therefore, a greater need for cooperative education*.

Its aim is to impart cooperative culture as the best model for establishing social relations and this requires a permanent educational effort with good intentions and the application of the cooperative precepts which are to be found in the Principles of the International Cooperative Alliance and the specific principles of the Mondragon Cooperative Group.

To this end, it has been proposed:

- To create effective didactic elements for training and informing cooperators, and

- To give specific courses in proportion to the cultural and professional level of the cooperator members.

Once the Basic Principles were defined, the activities aimed at permeating and extending cooperative education were centred on:

- Giving members, on a universal basis, a sense of cooperation as basic prerequisite so they can conscientiously take on their role as members.

- Developing courses for new members, for members of Social Councils, for management and members in general.

Annually, the educational needs are planned for the different Cooperatives in the Group, when the cooperatives so request, programming course throughout the year.

The subjects studied basically revolve around the following:

    1. A brief history of Cooperativism
    2. Don José María Arizmendiarrieta and his collaborators
    3. The internal organisation of a cooperative

4. The cooperative member

5. The Cooperative Principles of the Experience

6. The legal structure

7. The Mondragon Cooperative Group

8. The future of the cooperativism of the Mondragon Cooperative Group.

In any case, cooperative education is a subject which has not been developed with the same eagerness as other functions of a more practical nature, imposed by the specific nature and natural dynamism of the more pressing aspirations of companies.

The Group was built on an ideological cooperative fabric, but it may be that this is now somewhat worn, not because its precepts have been violated, but because although the key factors remain unchanged, as demonstrated by the Principles established only three years ago in 1987, they must be adapted so that in their application they maintain their original brilliance.

We are now treading a new stage with new actors, competitors in the market economy, to whom we must measure up to make our mark, without tarnishing or abandoning the essence of our Principles.

The Otalora Manor House in Aretxabaleta, Guipuzcoa; Cooperative and management training centre

"**W**hat should single out cooperativism is not so much the assimilation or faithfulness of a doctrine, but a form of behaviour in which the ends determine the quality and condition of the means. Cooperativism should be something fluid and which with time has to progress from the moment in which we recognise man as a perfectionable being, while trying to transform everything around him true to his destiny and vocation (J. Mª Arizmendiarrieta)".

7. THE FUTURE OF THE GROUP

Without doubt the unfinished task for the cooperatives participating in the *Mondragon Cooperative Experience* has always been the creation of the Group, and its configuration, in a state of permanent flux, has always been associated with the future.

This idea can be taken further by asserting that the future of the Group lies in having as its backdrop the challenge, only partially assumed, of overcoming the gap between different activities, cooperatives created, economic sectors covered and business cultures established in each part of the *Experience.*

It is a matter of developing a unitary idea, mutually enriching and capable of giving more solidity and guarantees to this group of entities which has to take on the uncertainties of a world in a state of permanent change, heading towards decidedly more competitive arenas.

From the start the cooperatives associated with Caja Laboral Popular have always been known as the Group. However the one hundred or so companies created, significant in terms of the figures we have seen, were never organised in a group in the sense most commonly accepted of this term, especially in the English speaking world.

Business groups are normally structured under one single management, be it one person or more, with a set of common strategies, a single social vocation and shared financial and economic responsibility to compensate for the unequal situations which occur and influence the framework of each part of the Group.

A set of companies which have in common the same source of finance, the same statutes and operating system, and which once a year attend the General Assembly of Caja Laboral Popular, which they have joined to expand the "club" of entities associated with CLP, is not just for these reasons a Business Group.

With different motivations and criteria, over the last ten years especially, an effort has been made to reach an acceptable level of intercooperation, as a prior phase to achieving the specific connotations of a group. The results, although progress has been made and in 1991 an acceptable level of consolidation may be obtained, are still not completely satisfactory. The outlook is positive and is stimulated from outside by a changing scenario which contains adjustment factors which have their most decisive expression in the new size of the market.

In this section of the book we shall summarise the reflections made, the process followed and the situation reached at the start of 1991 after the efforts made to consolidate the Mondragon Cooperative Group.

1) Initial difficulties

At the start the *Mondragón Cooperative Experience* did not take into account any determining factor to direct its activities towards the creation of an homogeneous business group.

The activities taken on originally: domestic appliances, casting and electronics, and later retailing, dairy products and machine-tools, clearly demonstrate that, with the breadth of the sectors selected and the scope of the technologies to be mastered, it was difficult to tackle them effectively with sufficient means to achieve a competitive, leading position outside the limited domestic market.

Today it is clear that the sectors in which the Group associated with CLP (which wants to become the Mondragón Cooperative Group) operates, are excessive and that the technological spread is very wide.

So when we want the reasons for consolidating the Group to be of a structural nature - producing economies of scale- and not ideological - just because they are cooperatives - our convictions are weakened because, with a few exceptions, the overall improvements are not clearly perceptible.

Moreover it should not be forgotten that the ideological discourse is ever less convincing and less frequent because the social environment has changed and other ideas have now come to the fore. On the other hand, industrial democracy, the key to the cooperative system, for basic decisions to be taken to shape its future, requires well founded arguments, clear concepts and clear evidence that participation in a new business group is going to provide more stability and greater economies in the future.

Stressing the original "sins" of the *Experience*, the limitations imposed at the start of the project cannot be forgotten: practically nothing remotely like what turns out to be necessary now was considered then.

Efforts were concentrated on the creation and success of the isolated stutterings of cooperatives such as Ulgor, Arrasate, Funcor, Lana, Urssa, San José Consumer Cooperative, and later Caja Laboral Popular, Lagun-Aro and Eskola Politeknikoa.

Only the key ideas had any element of future planning: work, saving, solidarity. No idea of a close knit group was designed to achieve internal cohesion.

The founder of the *Experience* cherished the barely expressed idea of extending the *Experience* along the road which the students of the Eskola Politeknikoa were creating. Therefore Ulgor, Arrasate, Copreci, Ederlan, Lana and, as a Mondragon projection, Urssa, are key cooperatives in the Group in that their founders and the main management team came from the Eskola.

These managers were going to be interpreters of Don José Maria Arizmendiarrieta's message in the companies, being not so erudite in cooperative legislation as in essential human and community company values.

The Group was like a business entity with a shapeless texture, with no models of reference, no links to related technology and not even basic or auxiliary services with which to establish some sort of interdependence. The teaching of the founder bore down on any decision and his teaching was not channelled through systems of economic or industrial orthodoxy, but based, rather, on ethical arguments.

With the creation of Ularco (now Fagor) there was a desire to tackle this problem, but the level of technological interdependence necessary for its scientific development was not reached, nor was supply adequately grouped as the markets for the products were different.

It is clear that the future of the *Experience* was based on specifically moral or sociological reasons, from which very few economic possibilities could be obtained as a structural guarantee for the future. However, the following could be said to be the most important objectives pursued by the organised grouping of cooperatives:

a) To develop a long term policy of foresight based on a Council of Directors who in turn would directly manage the cooperatives committed to the project.

b) To obtain ideal critical masses to create, in an efficient fashion, cooperatives such as Caja Laboral Popular and Lagun-Aro, which needed

MANAGERS OF THE NEW ORGANIZATION

Mongelos, Fco. Javier

Cancelo, Antonio

Catania, Jesús

capital to establish themselves, enough members, a committed loyal market, and cooperative management in harmony with the social model pursued.

c) To maintain efficiently vocational training centres to secure competent engineers, full of social ideals compatible with the cooperative system. These centres would, in turn, develop their course content to coordinate the capacities of these engineers, future members and managers with the growth of the companies.

d) To establish specific services in common or central services to develop general functions which could be assimilated by any cooperative: cooperative staff selection and evaluation, company medicine service, patents service, transport, promotion of new activities, computing services capable of being organised in common, etc. As can be seen, all of these are peripheral activities or at least do not affect the basic functions of the company, which are: to conceive, produce and sell.

e) By virtue of the ethical concepts of solidarity, common sense and in general, social sensibility, to develop a policy of matching wage levels and the application of profits so that all the workers in the cooperative grouping have the same economic capacity whichever cooperative they belong to and whatever profits they make, facilitating the transfer of staff between cooperatives as a key objective for optimising production factors.

These were the ideas being considered in the middle of the sixties, an effervescent period of creation, with the accent on transformation and magnanimously backed by an economic situation which was made this the decade of accelerated economic development in Spain.

The future was to be built on these assumptions, insofar as the backdrop clearly indicated the way and the protagonists of the Experience took pains to put them into practice, convinced as they now were that the companies, as companies placing the emphasis on people, were firmly consolidated, prestigious and economically efficient.

"At the start the Mondragón Cooperative Experience did not take into account any determining factor to direct its activities towards the creation of an homogeneous business group."

The initiatives to create cooperative groups only slowly came about as a plan for the future.

After the creation of Fagor in 1964 it was not until 1978 that Goilan was added, and little by little the future was laid out on the basis of creating a union of forces to serve society better, which was centred on the creation of employment in economic companies controlled by cooperative democracy.

The marvellous opportunities which Fagor took advantage of in the Alto Deba, the accelerated dynamism to achieve growth, the financial entities establishing financial cover and short and long term social benefits, were facing quite a comfortable and hopeful future.

Moreover, cooperativism, based on companies where the emphasis is on people, was not affected in the essence of its management, which was perfectly consolidated in each of the cooperatives. The general management of the local groups limited their activity, above all, to those functions which could be delegated with little effort as they did not have anything to do with the specific activities which distinguished each cooperative in the product-market relationship. The big difficulty arose when it came to grouping profits together and redistributing them amongst the cooperatives on the basis of the sum of wages. But this problem was alleviated by making this a gradual process, and some groups never achieved total pooling of profits following this path, stopping at 50 or 70%, and leaving a certain margin for providing incentives for personal effort, in the belief that too much equality in the distribution of profits, would have debased the collective effort.

All these attempts were, in the first half of the life of the Experience, vehicles for securing the future and goals which were always later overtaken by events. But they are undoubtedly evidence, providing lessons to be learned, that at the heart of the Experience no effort has been spared to secure, as far as possible, a comfortable future.

2) Rallying capabilities to consolidate the future

It was as a result of the crisis suffered from 1976 onwards due to the exaggerated and unexpected rise in the cost of fuel, that thoughts turned to the structural weakness of any business organisation run in isolation, with no financial, technological or commercial support.

This led, between 1978 (Goilan) and 1985 (Goikoa) to a series of initiatives to create the so-called local groups, in the image of the Fagor Group.

Fundamentally, there were two reasons behind the project which spurred it on.

On the one hand, the conviction in management circles that individual companies were incapable of solidly and securely tackling credible plans for development without a serious risk of jeopardising their future. On the other hand, there was the conviction that through the establishment of groups there were greater social, economic and, as a whole business prospects for promoting new initiatives, maintaining and creating new jobs and developing in each area an industrial policy sensitive to the labour market and its own economy.

The cession, on the part of the cooperatives, of part of their sovereignty to the incipient central services created, and to joint General Management, with autonomy always maintained in the last instance but with the capacity for coordination, was the step which, together with the development of the Group, harmonised future plans.

From 1975 to 1984 the economic scene had enormous influence and was the cause of much reflection on the orderly channelling of the future of the Group.

The Contract of Association with Caja Laboral Popular, which served to regulate social conduct and the structure of internal organisation, was one of the documents which laid the foundations, through its general acceptance, for the first ideas of an overall Group, still referred to as "associated with Caja Laboral Popular".

The size of all the cooperatives and the general crisis suffered led to Caja Laboral Popular itself, the key to the system due to its financial power at the service of the cooperatives in this period of depression, promoting the idea of the need to group together.

A model of intercooperation was created through the local groups, which added certain positive, dimensional factors resulting from the new situation, to this substantial and unique value.

However, the need to reexamine it in the light of political events was not long in coming: the death of General Franco (1975), new Spanish Constitution (1978), Statute of Basque Autonomy (1979), European Community Membership Agreement (1986) and the prospect of the removal of customs barriers for 1993.

There were other internal events of no lesser influence: the death of our founder (1976), the creation of local groups, as mentioned, the reduction from 70% of the resources applied by Caja Laboral Popular to the Group in 1962 to 25% in 1983 with increasing dedication to third parties who were not members; retirement of the Managing Director in 1987 and the Chairman in 1989, who had led the Caja from its birth, and, above all, the awareness of the need for change in the face of a new domestic market which was the product of a new political conception of Europe, involving the permanent and gradual reduction of customs barriers on the transfer of goods and services, people and capital.

These threatening yet stimulating changes led to the following reflections in 1982:

"a) Cooperativism has not spread sufficiently in institutional terms in the geographical area in which CLP operates to enable us to talk of a common situation in which CLP could have offered its financial management, without the need for looking beyond its members because of the lack of importance of its customers, their dispersion and their risk.

b) The singular nature of the cooperative phenomenon as a local exception, defined by prior association to CLP and the ideological vocation expressed in its legal documents and social conduct, establish in themselves basic yet restrictive relationships aimed at the creation of worker cooperatives in community and solidary terms.

c) The development of these relationships should be pursued gradually to secure:

= Socio-economic behaviour coherent with the intrinsic importance of the Experience.

= Efficient deployment of technological development based on the establishment of an industrial policy in specific technical areas, fully capable of being researched in depth.

" *It was as a result of the crisis suffered from 1976 onwards due to the exaggerated and unexpected rise in the cost of fuel, that thoughts turned to the structural weakness of any business organisation run in isolation, with no financial, technological or commercial support".*

= The harmonisation of a staff policy, through the readjustment of work forces with adequate transfers; the creation of management staff for optimum and solvent placement; cooperative training with a strong emphasis on the conduct desired of members.

= The organisation, insofar as possible, of sectorial ties, grouping together investment and management activities in technical and marketing areas, which surpass individual efforts, incapable now of emerging from a lamentable level of underdevelopment.

= The creation of support bodies in which to delegate specific parcels of power to channel and harmonise the general policy of the Group.

= The proposal and attainment in Political and Government Institutions of legal measures to promote the obstacle-free development of Cooperativism as a progressive and durable system.

These are the axes of a policy of change which, 25 years after the creation of the Experience, advises the adoption of a new and fresh form of conduct".

In this document the directives were established for the creation of the General Council and the Cooperative Congress, which were, in effect, developed later.

In 1983 stress was again placed on the advisability of developing a new *"industrial policy"*, aimed precisely at breaking the peripheral links in reality represented, in the face of external threats, by the ideological ties evoked in the social statutes, the norms of operation, the association with Caja Laboral Popular as a nexus of commitments and reciprocal support, and with Lagun-Aro for the organisation of a specific Social Security system of our own.

What was said, in short, was as follows:

*"1. **The disposition of management** to a single industrial policy is a key element. Conviction and a favourable attitude in the practical application of principles are an indispensable condition, without the support of which everything sought from different isolated positions is a mere theoretical posture. The introduction of an Industrial Policy depends on their attitude and without the determined support of management bodies neither its fair interpretation nor its consolidation would be possible.*

*2. **Sectorial Groups** are necessary to a coordinated Industrial Policy. From the point of view of business efficiency, big opportunities are being lost in organisation, market, innovation and representation by not joining forces with frameworks and institutions which together could attain a higher level of management and, in short, economic and social efficiency.*

*3. **The Cooperative Congress and the General Council** are pending bodies which are considered essential for the consolidation of an Industrial Policy. Once the Industrial Sectors which are susceptible to the creation of cooperatives have been selected, the approval of new start-ups, a control to avoid distortion in production, and the sanction of situations which have caused conflicts, should be channelled to project coherently united, economic and social activities.*

4. On the basis of entities whose sovereign will is based on people, it is necessary to find through pacts and agreements, solutions which due to the accumulation of financial power only serve companies with shareholders. It can therefore be deduced that to consolidate the Industrial Policy it is necessary to adopt a general agreement which, going beyond the necessarily schematic Contract of Association with Caja Laboral Popular, should progress towards specific spheres of collaboration: institutional, social, technical and Industrial Policy, the later probably being the less demanded, protected and tested."

With this backdrop, ideas were developed somewhat timidly for establishing the future of the Experience on firmer bases capable of securing, in a unitarian vision, not only ideological but more essentially entrepreneurial factors.

On 19th December 1984 the Basic Articles of the Congress of the Mondragon Cooperative Group and its General Council were approved, and two bodies were thus created, although still in an early phase, which were to be essential in starting an ordered and joint dialogue on the future of the Group, initiating debates on its internal organisation.

On the basis of this new situation, as precarious as any company in its infancy, the 1st Cooperative Congress was held in 1987.

It is clear that the documents approved were still based on ideological assumptions and did not yet tackle matters of a sectorial nature which could affect the business environment, the essence of which was the product and its market. Obviously this is where the future of our cooperatives will de decided.

The subjects covered in the Congress were as follows:

- The Basic Principles of the Mondragon Cooperative Experience.

- The Basic Regulations for the "Treatment of Social Capital"

- The Basic Regulations for the "Payment Differential"

- The Regulations for the "Bases for the Creation of the Intercooperative Solidarity Fund".

These basic regulations consolidated the cooperative principles, widened the payment differential and created a new, more committed, vehicle for finance, aimed especially at providing equity for new cooperatives or for those in crisis situations.

In the Congress the instrument for taking decisions was at hand, but the future of the Group, which began to be referred to as the **Mondragón Cooperative** Group, was not capable of tackling measures leading to the integration necessary to produce the advantages inherent in economies of scale, because opportunities based on technology and the market were not included.

One of the decisive steps behind the configuration of the Group on entrepreneurial lines, was developed on 19th to 21st October 1988 during the special days the Mondragon Cooperative Group held on the subject of "Facing Up to the European Economic Community".

It was necessary to stimulate a change in attitude to plan the future of the Group without resistance. Above all it was necessary to change the characteristics required to participate in the cooperative "club", all of which were of a social, legal or formal nature, in order to propose others of a entrepreneurial nature, capable of generating economies of scale and attaining sufficient dimension for the more competitive framework which the Economic Community heralded. In short, the threat that a new domestic market of 320 million inhabitants represented, was used to encourage the principal members in charge

n 19th December 1984 the Basic Articles of the Congress of the Mondragon Cooperative Group and its General Council were approved, and two bodies were thus created, although still in an early phase, which were to be essential in starting an ordered and joint dialogue on the future of the Group, initiating debates on its internal organisation."

of the cooperatives and redirect them to a more coherent vision of the circumstances which, although they proved no threat to the cooperative principles, would obtain fuller intercooperation from the cooperatives. This was in the belief that apparent formal uncommitted compliance with these principles would not necessarily lead to a strengthening of the Group, in entrepreneurial terms.

The debate concentrated, in practical terms, on the main sectors and its main theme was the analysis of the **Effect of the European Community and the Strategies to be Adopted** in ten production sectors: Casting and Forging, Capital Goods, Intermediate Goods, Machine-tools, Domestic Appliances, Wooden Furniture, Construction, Agriculture, Consumer and Finance.

The general dilemma which remained can be summarised as follows:

"In our desire to transform structures it is clear that when we established our companies we paid no heed to multinational consortiums, nor to the Single European Market.

We could not have done so, because when we started, amongst other things, the Treaty of Rome had not been signed. In any case this would not have changed anything.

The fact is that the products most important to the Group: domestic appliances, machine-tools and other capital goods, electronic and electro-mechanical components, plastics, wooden furniture, public works machinery, etc. etc., are in most cases also those favoured by the big multinationals, and now, in the new entrepreneurial confrontation which is on the horizon, we shall have to measure up to a completely different scenario which requires that we at least pause to ask the following questions.

Are there any specific products not favoured by large capitalist companies? Is it possible to find a market segment more accessible to worker cooperatives due to their capacity to adapt, taking advantage of their singular nature as community based companies? Would it, in any case, be possible to adapt our companies to a new product-market relationship scheme if we saw that there was a redoubt which had been scorned by, or was at least less accessible to, capitalist companies?

In principle it seems that these reflections indicate that many of our companies have passed with ease, due to their industrial structure and their position in competitive areas on an international scale, the point of no return, unless they are to change their products, for a new market, with new technology. It is clear that we must test our old adage that vitality is demonstrated by rebirth and adapting in time.

It has been calculated that at least 50% of the importance of our Group, especially industrial, is at this technical and marketing crossroads and that therefore we have reached the moment when we must find a way out in time to tackle this unquestionable challenge in time and in a determined fashion."

By way of summary, amongst others, the following ideas were gathered together on the future organisation of the Group:

"1. Speed up decision making.

2. Cede sovereignty from the Cooperatives to the Groups, centralising management decisions and giving General Management more decision-making power.

3. Cede sovereignty from the Groups and incorporated companies to the General Council of the Mondragon Cooperative Group, giving full executive capacity for strategic planning, human resources and new activities and strengthening its role in the establishment and execution of the management policy of the Group, including the selection of the sectors to be developed or written off.

4. Merge current Groups, establishing a maximum of 8 centres of decision and strategic planning, based on sectors to be given priority to.

5. Appoint a General Manager for each sector, to establish commercial networks, develop product ranges and draw up the strategic plan for the sector.

6. Encourage the General Council to analyze the possibility of promoting more development in the service sector in the heart of the Mondragon Cooperative Group."

In this situation of slow gestation it became clear that the future of the Group should be based on replacing the local groups, more on the basis of sociological criteria, with links which would increase market share, technological advances through Research and Development, economies of scale and even corporate image.

However, when it came to taking a decision, this had been a battle into which we had been forced and cornered by total acceptance of the democratic rules of the Group and its institutions.

Probably in this firmness to avoid change in addition to the intrinsic difficulties, the already consolidated organisations at local level along with the different size and efficiency of the different groups also played a part.

The theories established over 25 years in favour of the local groups were not easy to uproot and even though there were cases in which geographical location and type of products coincided - Debako, Urkide, Erein, Eroski - the future was not accessible at least spontaneously and rapidly, so it was necessary to trust to the "lessons of time" and catalyse our efforts with energy, showing the unquestionable advantages capable of offering the sum of the essential advantages of enterprises, and swaying opinions towards favouring the new ideas which would shape the Group.

This was the situation in the run-up to the 2nd Cooperative Congress. The aims sketched for this event revolved around an idea which had germinated thanks to the fruitfulness of dialogue: We had to progress from being a *"Sociological Experiment to a Business Group"*.

On 1st and 2nd December 1989, on the occasion of the 2nd Cooperative Congress, those attending were presented with a proposal for a new concept for constructing the future of the Group.

For the groups to be sure of success they had to meet certain conditions capable of providing greater efficiency by:

a) Keeping close technological links so as to be able to carry out a common policy of research and development.

b) Creating, constructing and providing homogenous goods for the market, offering them through the same commercial channels to the segments which require them.

c) Obtaining technical quality equally approvable, so that the Group as a whole is not harmed by partial and isolated deficiencies.

d) Promoting and using a principal trademark so that the products offered are universally identifiable.

e) Obtaining, as a result of grouping, a large share in supply and in the market, greater capacity to respond to demand, and greater capacity to generate economies and to promote the general potential of the Group.

This was the prevailing idea which most clearly expressed the future direction to be taken by the Mondragon Cooperative Group.

Other subjects covered between the 1st Congress and the 3rd Congress to be held at the end of 1991 were as follows:

- The Basic Regulations for the creation of an"Intercooperative Education and Promotion Fund (FEPI)".

- The Basic Regulations for the "Organisations of theCooperative Groups.

- The Basic Regulations for the "Creation of Employment".

After the second Congress the Mondragon Cooperative Group began to formulate a new theory which required a modification in the way the Group was seen and which shall have a great deal of influence in the future.

3) The sectorial formulation to defend the Group's mission and future

The Group has a future as long as it fulfils its mission over so many years as the trustee of the social model applied to companies in the *Mondragón Cooperative Experience.*

This future will come to an end when the Group can no longer fulfil its mission, as at that moment it will have begun another which is not that which it tackles and pursues today.

This can only be said without examining what might occur beyond the foreseeable future, in the firm conviction that at each moment companies have to respond effectively to problems which may arise.

When dealing with the future of the Group, there are therefore three main ideas capable of generally laying the path to be followed in the near future, bearing in mind that the longer term is subject to outside circumstances, on which we have no control: thus it cannot be reduced to foreseeable proportions.

The three main ideas are as follows:

- The **mission** on which the Group is based, to maintain the identity of the Experience.

- The **basic organisation**, capable of providing the backbone for competitively tackling a wider market.

- The **functions** of the Group's own financial institutions as the necessary agents for fulfilling the aforementioned objectives.

We shall now summarise the key elements for planning the future pursued by the Group.

The Mission of the Group

The 2nd Congress of the Mondragón Cooperative defined this as follows:

"The scenario has changed and various events, amongst others, are now occurring which affect the fundamental aspects of the initial mission of moral connivance, because the market is larger, competitiveness is sharper and the size of companies has taken on other proportions, precisely to tackle the effects of a new situation. A call is now made for offensive action, based on the hypothesis of a financial grouping, corporation or holding, which will result in a reduction of unit costs, an increase in competitiveness, access to greater market share, capacity for investment in new technology, in an audacious effort to increase profitability, keeping external threats at bay and consolidating the future.

On the basis of this analysis, it is worth citing the challenges provided by Spain's imminent membership of the Economic Community in a social, economic and political context. The **mission** of the Group shall respond to the following assumptions:

• *The cooperative experience embodied by the Mondragón Cooperative Experience, in socioeconomic terms in the framework of a company, takes as its mission the production and sale of goods and services, adopting in its internal organisation democratic methods for the selection of management and distributing the material and social wealth produced, for the benefit of all the workers and the community in which its activities take place.*

• *To achieve the objectives of the mission of the Cooperative Group, it should operate from a competitive stance, generating and controlling human and financial resources to attain progressive and harmonious development.*

Alfonso Gorroñogoitia
Jesús Larrañaga
José M.ª Ormaechea

THE FOUNDERS TODAY

• *Support services shall be provided, economies of scale generated, innovation and research promoted and the means necessary established to enable the Group to attain corporate leadership in the Single European Market in those sectors chosen as those of preferential interest by the bodies of the Group.*

• *In compliance with the Basic Principles approved by the 1st Cooperative Congress, the Group shall facilitate the human and professional advancement of its worker-members, for whom it shall provide economic wellbeing and a quality of life and work in harmony with the exercising of solidarity and balanced long term entrepreneurial development."*

On the basis of these hypotheses, a synthesis of the social conduct followed by the Mondragon Cooperative, the following strategic actions should be promoted in the heart of the Cooperative Experience:

1) An increase in basic capacity, offering greater opportunity for consolidating and developing an economic and social project with a wide entrepreneurial scope.

2) Economic optimisation, adding up market capacity and reducing unit costs.

3) Organising larger homogenous units, by a redistribution of the model of cooperative groups to strengthen product and market opportunities.

4) Developing R + D as an essential factor in the generation of value added, to compensate for technological backwardness and to adapt the groups to the new competitive scenario.

5) Carry out sectorial development with regard to the basic cooperatives, through turnover, export capacity, number of workers, profitability and technological autonomy.

As for Caja Laboral Popular, the key to the creation and development of the Group, its strategies for the three year period 1990-1992 were established, with its mission defined as follows:

"Caja Laboral Popular is part of the Mondragón Cooperative Group, and, like the Group, is dedicated to the reform of companies, to make them democratic and participatory.

Its social and economic activities shall be limited to the Basque Country; however, it may operate outside these geographical confines to achieve its objectives of economically strengthening the region, of serving the Associated Group with more means and reaffirming itself as a solid, competitive and viable economic institution.

"It is quite clear therefore that the purpose of the Group in the future is to respect the basic principles which inspired its creation, and to search for the best way to adapt to changing circumstances."

It shall maintain the hypotheses defined by the Mondragón Cooperative Group and actively participate in the adaptation of the Group to the new European scenario which the Group must tackle.

It shall provide preferential financial services to its associated cooperatives, and shall support and promote the creation of cooperative employment using the economic resources available, collaborating in the recovery of associated cooperatives in difficulty and ensuring that the capital gains generated through its activities are reinvested in society giving prevalence to community over individual development.

Likewise, it shall provide financial services at the market rate for Other Companies and Household Economies, always with the aim of creating wealth and generating employment for society".

It is quite clear therefore that the purpose of the Group in the future is to respect the basic principles which inspired its creation, and to search for the best way to adapt to changing circumstances.

Basic Organisation

For the practical application of the hypotheses described an Organisational Project has been developed as an open platform constituting the first step in a general analysis of the organisation.

Eight divisions have been selected, on the basis of the following advantages:

a) Taking advantage of the value added of cooperatives grouped through strategic management aimed at responding to market needs.

b) Achieving a higher market share via the combination of the products offered by the cooperatives in the division.

The divisions chosen are as follows:

- Finance
- Capital Goods
- Car Components
- Domestic Appliance Components
- Industrial Components and Services
- Construction
- Food and Retailing
- Household

As far as the Institutional Organisation which serves as the legal framework for the new concept of companies established in Divisions and Sectorial Groups is concerned, advances have been made towards the creation of a single support body. However, the process cannot be materialised right away because the "culture" created in each working community has consolidated the tendency to develop an autonomous policy in economic, product and market functions, which is so deeply rooted that only clear evidence of a new situation and the "lessons of time" will get things moving in the direction of attaining a unitarian concept of management for the Group.

It is a matter of perfecting the Bases of operation for the Congress and General Council, giving the Congress, as a temporary measure, the functions of a General Assembly; the Permanent Committee of the Congress, the function of control and support for the General Council, and the General Council, executive capacity.

The General Council will be made up of the top executives of the divisions created and the managers of the Central Departments which will serve all sectors in the following fields:

- Social Management - Human Resources

- Technological Development - Research + Development

- Financial Management

- International Relations and Corporate Image

To strengthen the Group's image logos and trademarks will be unified, emphasising:

- Fagor in the industrial sector

- Caja Laboral Popular in the financial sector, and

- Eroski in the retail sector.

The Function of the Financial Institutions

The Group has always sought cohesion through those institutions which have offered a service in common for all the cooperatives and their members.

Due to lack of direct links, often impossible in the restrictive legal framework of cooperativism, entities like Caja Laboral Popular, with its Business Division, Lagun-Aro, Ikerlan and Eskola Politeknikoa have been, due to the quality and importance of their roles, the ones who have kept alive the concept of a Group bound together in functional aspects, but not so in its essential roots.

In the future, Caja Laboral Popular and Lagun-Aro especially, have an essential role to play, to such an extent that if they only adopted an inward-looking position, with no commitment to the cooperative project for the future, this project would not be viable.

The overall financial capacity of the Group at the end of 1990 totalled 500,000 million

PROPOSAL FOR THE ORGANIZATION OF THE MONDRAGON COOPERATIVE GROUP

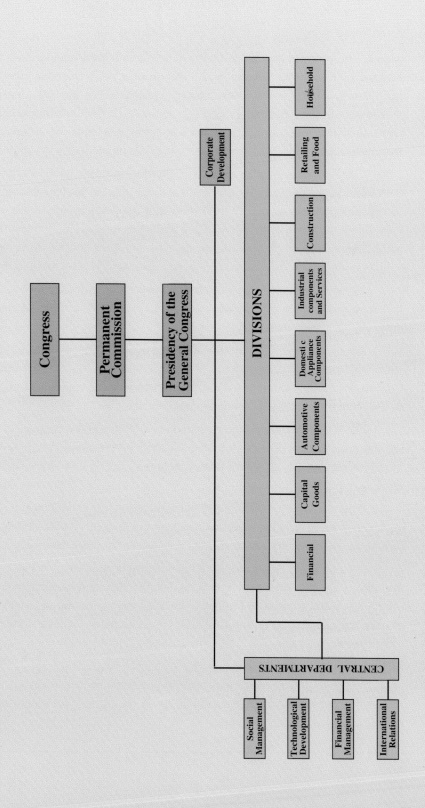

pesetas. This potential does not just serve to save crisis situations, like those happily overcome between 1975 and 1985, but also helps in the prudent and responsible exercise of strengthening the technological sectors chosen as the key elements for the Group. The mediation of Caja Laboral Popular is decisive in starting up a technologically and institutionally complex new activity and a deterrent mission can be undertaken to move away from those sectors thought to be risky, beyond or unsuitable for the system.

Caja Laboral Popular has perfectly defined its **mission** and in this context, the future of the Group is protected by its cooperative financing, in perfect harmony with the idea of *"planning its management at the highest level of efficiency in the interest of the collective, combining in turn the interests of the different working communities to make them more compatible and fruitful and through its activities compensating for the partial or temporary limitations suffered by each group"*. Don José Maria Arizmendiarrieta.

As far as Lagun-Aro is concerned, on the basis of its Strategic Plan, it must face up to the future with the aim of providing cover for its members and trying to organise itself along the lines of European models of social cover.

In a Europe, ever more united and shared by its citizens, ever more European, it will be harder, and even absurd, not to adapt to the Social Security systems defended by the different Countries in which non-contributory benefits will increase and Budget support will be essential to a reduction in company contributions.

If it is true that superior cultures end up by removing all evidence of inferior systems, the time is then ripe to plan a future Social Security system of our own, linked to and approved by the future plans established for Europe, both in its financial system, as in the model and the scope of its benefits.

From the same financial point of view, essential for the future development of the Group, the idea of including capitalist companies in the general plan has been established. To date, two such operations, of a certain financial and social scope, have been carried out.

This new strategy, full of apparent contradictions with the *"principles"* and the *"mission"* described herein, can be explained in terms of the need to achieve optimum economies of scale to make the cooperatives profitable, and even more so the sectors which emerge from the grouping of the cooperatives. Consolidation in Europe, and moreover, the desire to attain sufficient critical size in terms of production time, are going to lead to vigorous actions which would be impossible to apply through the promotion of cooperatives alone.

It is going to be necessary to establish the minimum conditions to carry out this new strategy for purchasing companies and to increase our capacity for supply and the economies of scale produced by each operation.

The clash on the basis of the social criteria contained in the "principles" and in the "mission" establishes the guidelines to be followed, not just in purely technical terms. Otherwise, the fact of having some self-employed workers and others "employed" by them, will not be easy to explain nor will it be coherent.

In any case, the plan is to create a Holding Company which will carry out these initiatives, constituting a *"appropriate tool to back the financial investment necessary to launch or control companies in accordance with the strategic decisions of the Group"*.

This Company, which will be owned, mainly, by the financial institutions of the Group, will be controlled by its size, profitability and the fact that, above all, it responds to the totally complementary strategic objectives for which shares in companies not organised as companies with the emphasis on people were acquired.

Through this Holding Company the scope of these companies shall be kept within reasonable limits so that this solution does not lose all proportion and seriously affect the organisation and principles which the Group has solemnly declared that it wishes to maintain and practice.

4) New Horizons

Whatever the Mondragon Cooperative Group is to be in the future necessarily depends on the attitude of the men who are progressively taking over from the first generation of leaders.

Society has changed very quickly in the last 35 years, opening up new horizons within the framework of which it will be necessary to provide an answer to the questions posed on coexistence and individual freedom. Fundamental projects, at least formally, no longer bear any resemblance to those through which the founders aspired to reform companies as a formula for emancipation and self-realization.

Neither is the economic scenario in any way similar to that of the first years of the Experience, because international links have grown, with a wide increase in cultural similarities, through which competitiveness, the market and technical professionalism make new demands. Strictly moral aspirations are left to one side because they are replaced by respect for privacy and individual advancement, in coherence with the options of others who, with the same degree of expectation, direct their own future.

Mondragon Cooperativism was created to satisfy and elevate the level of wellbeing, through the modification and the optimum use of forces which come together in business. It was necessary to transfer sovereignty from those who provided capital to those who provided their labour on a daily basis in communities where the emphasis was on people. This has been an important contribution which, in addition, has been socially and economically successful. There are few members who would abandon this concept because they consider it a privilege and an efficient means for overcoming the social tensions in the organised framework of companies.

The system created by the *Experience* is, in essence, highly capable of adaptation, and its own mechanisms of adjustment would have to be modified very little for the idea of companies with the emphasis on people to continue to be valid in the face of any changes which may result from the new situation derived from Spain's membership of the European Economic Community.

It would be difficult for any other organisations, based on other institutional models, to be in a better condition to take on the new socioeconomic situation sensitive to the uninterrupted advance of technology in which, once again, man will play the most valuable and decisive role.

Solidarity and labour shall not lose their value, and they shall always be irreplaceable resources for securing community development; and they cannot be sidestepped, because their acceptance, generously assumed, contains the real guarantees for developing the innovation of unceasing and productive companies.

We continue to place our faith, as convinced as ever, in the companies where the emphasis is on people which created the Experience, sure of the fact it is the best organisational answer for social coexistence in communities of demanding citizens who aspire to greater levels of wellbeing, and to share this with the rest.

"Today, after several years and having achieved an appreciable level of development, and at the same time with new forces, both internal and external, on which to count, it is more than just a new urge to reconsider the need for a restructuring to meet new horizons and in the awareness of possibilities which may have seemed utopian to us some years ago. Let us not confuse restructuring with oversight or the abandonment of human and social values which are untouchable, insofar as the Cooperative Experience was conceived as an element of human and community progress, which nobody would be prepared to abandon. But, on the other hand, we are all more or less prepared for our process of promotion to accelerate and increase so that, for us, new times mean new options for effective humanism. The natural rights and aspirations of man guide our Experience. The response to and compliance with these are our goals. Our cooperativism is based on solidary humane men and is ideal for combining and synchronising personal and community advancement, coherently establishing short and long terms actions, freedom and social justice". (J. Mª Arizmendiarrieta)

Fotomechanics
IGARA, S.A.

Filmsetting
PHOTO LINE

Printing
Lit. DANONA, S. COOP.

Design, Coordination
and Illustrations
GENERAL COUNCIL MCC

Legal Deposit
SS. 229-92

● January 1993